NOTES FROM

A JAZZ LIFE

Digby Fairweather

NOTES FROM

A JAZZ LIFE

with illustrations by
Peter Manders and
Humphrey Lyttelton

northway
publications

Published by Northway Publications
39 Tytherton Road, London N19 4PZ, UK
www.northwaybooks.com

Edited by Ann Cotterrell

Cover design by Stewart Aplin, Aplin Clark, London EC1

Cover photos by Alpha Photovisual Ltd, London N12

The publishers acknowledge with thanks the kind permis-
sion of Peter Manders to use his illustrations on pages 14,
25, 30, 58, 65, 75, 86, 101, 106, 114, 134, 150, 168, 169,
181 and the back cover, and Humphrey Lyttelton for the use
of his illustration on page 130.

A CIP record for this book is available from the British
Library.

ISBN 0 9537040-1-7

First published 2002

Printed and bound in Great Britain by Bookmarque Ltd,
Croydon, Surrey.

Contents

1.

first valve down

In 1946 Rochford's most visible landmark was a tall chimney towering protectively over a sprawling friendly hospital. It still is. Though the hospital is gone now, its chimney still stands like a guardian over the industrious Essex market town below. And it was in a crowded ward somewhere beneath this workaday monument that – with hundreds of other postwar babies – I was born, one year after the Second World War was over. In the dance halls, jitterbugging had made the journey across the Atlantic to Britain. Frank Sinatra and Rita Hayworth were the cinema's premier heart-throbs and Crosby, Hope and Lamour were on the 'Road to Utopia'. Of all this excitement I was, of course, completely unaware.

In fact, I decided to arrive a month late and remember my mother Ena telling me that while she was lying in considerable discomfort awaiting the reluctant arrival of her only son, she listened regularly to the BBC Light Programme's 'Stand Easy' show hosted by Charlie Chester and one early April morning heard a seasonal rendition of 'It Might As Well Be Spring' from Rogers and Hammerstein's 'State Fair'. As a tribute to Charlie for easing a little of the discomfort, Charles was added to my first two names, Richard and John. And their owner, conceived somewhere between VE night and

Hiroshima, finally appeared a minute or so before mid-day on April 25th 1946.

For the first twelve years of my life we lived in nearby Hockley. My father, John, had been a piano and cello teacher before the war but by the time I was born, he was a successful portrait photographer in Southend. Away from his camera, though, John's most durable pride and joy was his gramophone. Mounted in a shiny oak cabinet, it boasted a lightweight Leak pickup and turntable with big speakers mounted in concrete in a door-frame. His collection of classical 78s was kept in a mahogany cabinet, eight feet long. Then, when LPs came along in the early 1950s, John's 78 pick-up (right of the turntable) was speedily joined by a second to the left, with an expensive diamond stylus for LPs. And once it arrived I was encouraged to dig into his 78 collection as well as take over the right hand pickup! So all by myself I could find and replay music by Prokofiev, Elgar, Britten and particularly Walton's 'Belshazzar's Feast' with its challenging introduction for trombones. The passage where Belshazzar is slain by an avenging God, 'Mene, mene tekel upharsin' – 'thou art weighed in the balance and found wanting' – sounded as spine-chilling as anything from Hammer Studios. But it was in 1955 that one of my father's musical friends brought around a stout wind-up gramophone with silven metal soundbox pickup, needles to spare, and a pile of 78 records. 'Richard may as well have these,' he said, consigning the frivolous music of youth to his past. And with that sentence he helped alter the course of my musical life.

I carried the wind-up gramophone to our downstairs spare-room and stacked the 78s on a table nearby before beginning a voyage of discovery. And as I lifted the heavy pick-up to the running-in board of each old disc, I was exploring the popular music of a generation before. But the records I liked best were the jazz ones: Red Nichols, Joe Daniels and George Scott-Wood's Six Swingers. There was dance music on the radio too and plenty of other temptations to slum it down Tin Pan Alley. Two great musicals, 'Singin' in the Rain' and

'Daddy Long Legs' (starring Fred Astaire and Leslie Caron) both put in late appearances at a tiny local cinema in nearby Rayleigh. And at the moment in 'Daddy Long Legs' when I saw Fred swinging hard behind what to me looked like an enormous drum set, I realised that that was what I wanted. I was born to be a drummer!

By the age of ten, I had a yen for the trumpet as well as drums. Another film was partly responsible: 'It's Great to Be Young', starring Cecil Parker as a jazz-hating headmaster and the immortal Sir John Mills as a jazz-loving music teacher whose pupils rebel when he is dismissed for over devotion to his subject. In this film, Sir John both mimes as a trumpet player (to a headlong soundtrack by Humphrey Lyttelton and his Band) and rackets through a convincing version of 'Original Dixieland One-Step' on a pub piano. Such influences propelled me further towards jazz.

Trips around Southend junkshops brought fascinating discoveries too: an old violin with tatty bow, a wooden framed snare drum minus snare, a mandolin, an old guitar. Even a battered case suggesting musical contents was a treasure chest to raid. Best of all, though, were the music shops. Nowadays, guitars, drums, keyboards and amplifiers dominate the view but back then – at the sunset of the swing era – you could peer longingly through the glass at serried ranks of saxophones, trumpets, trombones, accordions, double-basses and drums in dozens of different designs and varying states of repair. But it was always the trumpet that held a special attraction. How, I was beginning to wonder, could you produce such challenging sounds from curved tubing, a single small mouthpiece and only three valves?

Later my attentions homed in to two shops in a side road at the top of Southend High Street. The first, run by Harry Strauss Senior, frequently had musical instruments in the window and, most thrillingly, one day, an old E-flat tenor horn. This wonderful-looking instrument might not have been as seductive as a trumpet, but it had all the principal qualifications: a big brass bell, lots of intriguing tubing and those three obligatory valves. I knew instantly that I wanted it more than anything else and in December 1959 the horn came back to be hidden for Christmas.

'You can practise for just five minutes a day,' said Ena.

The result was that, within a week or two, with the help of a tutor book, I could produce first a note, then a scale and on Christmas morning this was a source of surprise to John Fairweather, who didn't appear to know that his son had been training in secret. I had started down the brass track.

One day in 1959, my father drove his small family along the country roads towards Paglesham, a rural Essex village whose population then amounted to no more than three hundred, close to the River Roach, a seawater inlet from the Crouch and the North Sea. Near the village, we drove off the road, down a winding country lane and onto empty farmland, until to the left we saw a driveway and at its end an old rambling weatherboard Essex farmhouse.

'It's called Stannetts,' John explained. 'I'm thinking about buying it. What do you think?'

Behind this glorious house, a great apple orchard was in full bloom and as we drove down a muddy drive to the door, cattle grazed in the meadow alongside and, two or three fields away, the thin silver streak of a river glinted in the sun.

'Where's the nearest neighbour?' asked Ena.

'About a mile away,' said my father, wielding an enormous door-key, 'back by the road.' His key saw us through a once imposing front door and into a front hall full of hay. There were no light switches, and lots of slim-legged harvester spiders shook convulsively in their webs as our unexpected entry disturbed their peace of years.

'The house was built by someone called Adam de Stanflete,' John continued, 'three hundred years ago. He had his own creek, Stannetts Creek, and that's still there too, down the end of the track and across the meadow. The house was divided into two cottages – see that partition? But we can turn it back into one home. It'll be marvellous.'

Ena was far from sure: after all, there were no neighbours at all. My principal objection was to the army of spiders in every room. But, shored up by John's enthusiasm, we started to enjoy his transformation of this old nine room mansion. As evenings fell, he worked by the light of a tilly-lamp: clearing hay, scraping old paint, building a sink unit of hardboard, and knocking down partitions dividing the two halves of the house. No mains electricity came anywhere near, so a generator was installed which puttered into action, turning our first light on after a ten second wait. No mains drainage either (so we needed a septic tank) and no mains water, so we had to revive the garden well.

'Now then,' said Mr Cardy, the farm foreman who had kept a friendly eye on our activities from day one. 'You do know, don't you, Mr Fairweather, that an American soldier was blown into the well and killed in the recent conflict?'

My father looked apprehensive as he primed an old hand-pump in the garden, and especially after the water poured out scarlet.

'Don't you worry, Mr Fairweather,' said Mr Cardy with wicked joviality. 'I'm sure you had rust in the town too?'

My father installed an electric pump to take water to an attic tank and a coke fired Aga stove in the kitchen fireplace. When it was lit for the first time with charcoal a family of wild bees reluctantly vacated the hive of crenellations in the mantelpiece above. Outside there were two privies: a one-seater in its own tall wooden cabin, for solo trips – and a full three-seater for Sunday morning family outings.

Conquering my father's initial reluctance, we acquired a television set too. But after the first few hours of viewing, John decided that the new acquisition posed a threat to serious music listening and that we should have a separate television room upstairs right next to the bathroom. This was fine except that – due to the eccentric mechanics of our household electro-water supplies – every time you flushed the lavatory the television turned itself off in silent protest.

During the war, German pilots had dropped their bombs at the mouth of the Thames before heading home. Near to Stannetts were several bomb-craters – now green-edged ponds by which wild ducks and drakes built their nests – and in our orchard only the floor of a barn remained after a bomb had blown it to pieces, taking a lot of Stannetts' roof off in the process. Through the old wooden gate at the top of our drive, a track led to the boundary of great green meadows where church bells could be heard on Sundays. Walk across the meadows and you reached the old river bank dropping down to a still stretch of water. This was Stannetts Creek where marsh birds gathered and, from time to time, herons hauled themselves slowly skyward.

Our new home offered gentle, unsolved mysteries. A secret tunnel was said to stretch from the River Roach three fields away; smugglers escaped the excisemen by using this concealed route. And once we found a false-bottomed cupboard at floor-level in our sitting room but all that seemed to lie beneath it was sand. Only once or twice in our twenty years there do I remember ghostly moments. On one occasion, I woke up in the night to hear discordant unearthly music coming from the piano in our music room downstairs. What to do? Pull the covers over my head and pray? Certainly not, I was determined to see our ghost for myself! So down the stairs I tiptoed, the discords growing nearer and louder. Our piano room was at the end of the downstairs hall and the light switch was behind the door. So I would have to view my ghost in his natural habitat of darkness. Never mind, over the top now! Into the darkened piano room with eyes half-closed and flip myself behind the door and then, on with the light. But the musical ghost was just our family cat, strolling the keyboard.

In the country I could play my tenor-horn – and later the trumpet too – at any hour of day or night, without neighbours knocking. One early morning option was to play to the cattle in our neighbouring pastureland. As morning mists cleared, and the disembodied heads and trunks of herds of bullocks were slowly re-connected to their legs in the dawning morning light, I would take my trumpet outside and try out some jazz. The young herd would trot across the meadow and stand in line to listen to the music, heads on one side. Then, in unison, they all would pee.

Only once, years later, was there a human reaction. I had spent half an hour blowing at full power to Count Basie's record 'Sixteen Men Swinging' and 'Stereophonic'. Minutes after the cacophony had subsided, three hikers with rucksacks knocked at our front door. 'Excuse us please,' they said to Ena, 'but we thought we heard Morris dancers. Are they performing?'

For twenty years this beautiful timbered country house and its surrounds fostered all my jazz aspirations. By the river, in and among the salt-marshes, I heard echoes of Bix Beiderbecke, Jack Teagarden, Louis Armstrong and their jazz children. Listening in the silence of the country night I heard a million sculptured jazz choruses singing in the spheres. Forever, just as Hoagy Carmichael had his, this would be my own 'moon country'.

In 1959 nothing less than Paglesham's annual produce and flower show sealed my love of jazz forever. Our show was held in a meadow with a grand tent in which contestants vied for 'best flower arrangement', 'biggest marrow' and other coveted awards. Outside there were sideshows: bowling for the pig, coconut shies, hoop-la and much besides. It all made for a merry day. But just as we were about to make our way home in the late afternoon, a rumour spread. 'There's to be a jazz band in the tent tonight!' So back we came, in the evening light, down the long track from Stannetts. This was hardly Birdland – or even the newly-opened Ronnie Scott's up in London's Soho! But tables and chairs had been set out in the marquee, a rickety upright piano had arrived and, most sophisticated of all, shiny books of matches had been set on the tables – a wonderful jazz club touch, I thought, and very worldly.

Soon after, four young men walked in. One handsome dark boy that I vaguely recognised sat down at the piano: this was 'Dirk' Wood, the son of our neighbour Derek Wood. Next to him, another young man took a trumpet from its case: I heard them call him Alan. A third hauled in a bass, made from what looked like a wooden water barrel. And last of all came a drummer, carrying a set of loosely assembled traps: crackly three-inch snare drum (in stylish turquoise green) and cymbals bigger than I'd ever seen in my life. They must have cost pounds! These four young men set up their instruments, warmed up and, as the evening was coming on, lit up the gloaming with their opening fanfare. Truthfully I can't remember how they sounded. But that sunny evening, within four bars, they converted me for life to the music they had already learned to love.

One day, a few weeks later, I was standing outside our local tavern, the Plough and Sail. Perhaps I'd lost interest in the conversation and wandered out. But then, amazingly, I heard the strains of 'St Louis Blues' through the fresh night air. So what should I do but follow the music? Away from the lights of the pub, and along a muddy track below tall elm trees swaying in the breeze, to Derek Wood's manor house. Framed in a double doorway, the same four young men played, silhouetted in bright electric light, and I stood motionless. Will they notice if I creep in through the french doors left half ajar in the heat? No, it seems, if I take it steady and quietly: yes, I can creep in gently now, yes, yes, ok! I'm in. I'm in! In the midst of the swirling music from the trumpet, thrashing drums, piano and near audible tub-bass. In the midst of a jazz band! At last.

Over the weeks to come, despite their seniority of several years, these young musicians allowed me to join them to play their drums and to listen to music. Dirk had acquired the latest, hippest records and everything I heard I loved immediately. But there was one moment when I knew the music I was hearing was absolutely right. This was Louis Armstrong's 'Back o' Town Blues'. Four bars past Billy Kyle's piano introduction, the wild call of Louis' trumpet drew me in. I knew this was exactly the way that blues, jazz and the instrument I loved were all meant to sound.

From 1958 I had attended Southend High School for Boys (free musical instruments and tuition) taking up violin, then moving quite rapidly to the more jazz-friendly clarinet, although the music studies at school were classically-based. Buying my first LP required a major decision following plenty of research. I went to a jazz-loaded record shop in Southend and made my way to the counter. Why did record-shop proprietors always look so big? And bored? But plucking up courage, I presented a handful of LPs, 'Can I listen to this? And this? And maybe this?'

Then, out of the blue, I found a green shiny cover with splashes of colour: 'Great Jazz Brass' on RCA Camden with one track each by (amongst others) Louis Armstrong, Bix Beiderbecke, Buck Clayton, Muggsy Spanier and Jack Teagarden. The choice was made. Back home, fantastic technicolour jazz landscapes opened up: Armstrong and Teagarden mugging on 'Rocking Chair', Beiderbecke flashing from 'Barnacle Bill the Sailor' to create a silver streak of lightning solo, Clayton's reflective 'Buckin' the Blues' with John Collins' wonderful guitar entry, Spanier's Ragtimers' 'That Da Da Strain' filling my senses to the last triumphant cadence and finally, 'That's a Serious Thing!' with Teagarden's lazy vocal and gift-boxed trombone chorus.

From that day, record-buying was a lifelong bug. Beyond the shop of Harry Strauss Senior stood another, run by his son. My second LP came from Harry Strauss Junior and his weekly acquisitions were more tempting than bones to a hungry dog. Though he never smiled, nor offered more than an abrupt 'OK', he provided an informal pawnshop facility too.

'Mr Strauss, you know that marvellous new 'Jazztime USA' you've just put in the window?'

'Mmh.'

'Well, I've got this 12 inch LP here plus this 10 inch one. You've had them before I know, but do you think ....'

'Go on then ...!'

And out I would walk with a brand-new record. A week or two later Harry would, without a smile, swap back again and as a result his shop became my jazz university. But later, in 1968, I came back from two years at Ealing Technical College to find that both the Strauss shops had been flattened under an appalling new concrete precinct. Harry Junior had died soon after that happened, within six months of his father. I miss them both after forty years and dream of that wondrous shop: Harry Junior, miraculously young again, is still behind the counter, smiling welcome this time, and surrounded by dozens of previously undiscovered jazz records.

I was also a regular visitor to Southend Central Library where I found Milton 'Mezz' Mezzrow's technicolour *Really the Blues* and, soon after, Louis Armstrong's *Satchmo: My Life in New Orleans*, the story of a young simple man meeting life at its most rough-and-tumble with almost saintly fortitude. Then came Billie Holiday's *Lady Sings the Blues* (which it was hard to find anything but dismal) and, much more charismatically, Eddie Condon's incomparable *We Called it Music* and *Treasury of Jazz*. All of these I took back to my father's studio in Weston Road, devouring their contents in an underground room – along with the jazz sections of his collected *Gramophone* magazines. Occasionally he would pick up one of these books and gently 'tut tut'. After returning from the library one day with Alan Lomax's *Mr Jelly Roll* I was always very glad that he didn't turn up page 48. Check it for yourself!

By now, however, I knew what I wanted more than anything. I had, as Louis Armstrong put it, a 'terrible urge' to play the trumpet.

***

One Sunday lunchtime, a family friend called Fred Walker was drinking with us at the Plough and Sail. Fred had moved up from trumpet to french horn and mentioned that he still had his old trumpet at home. My attention was caught with the power of a man-trap and I pulled Ena's elbow urgently.

'Please! Ask him if I could borrow it! Please!'

'Certainly,' said Fred in response to Ena's request. 'I'll remember to bring it next week.'

I didn't know if he would, and spent the next week in a fever of anticipation. Sleep was almost out of the question. Come Sunday morning, with two hours to opening time, I was in torment. 'Go on,' said Ena, understandingly. 'I'm sure he won't mind if you ring and remind him.'

It took two seconds to get to the phone.

'Yes, I'm bringing it with me.'

To celebrate, I snatched up my battered tenor-horn to blow along with Humphrey Lyttelton's record 'It Makes my Love Come Down', its trumpet-breaks played into a glass tumbler. Pretty soon, I thought, I'd be doing that, just like my idol!

That lunchtime, at the pub, Fred Walker had at his feet the square black case, silver-locked and containing the B-flat trumpet. In a second, there was the thrill of unlocking the catches, then opening the lid, a tangy whiff of valve oil and the shine of the trumpet as I lifted it from its seating! As my parents toasted Fred and other friends, the trumpet case was opened again, then shut, then re-opened to check the treasure inside. At last, we made the triumphant parade home down the track to Stannetts, disturbing the peaceful countryside with brassy outbursts. By the time we'd reached the front door, I had 'When the Saints Go Marching In' ready for a country airing. Just like Louis Armstrong's – but in another time, another space, another hemisphere – my boyhood dream had come true.

From then I lived each moment vividly, charged by the electricity of this music and, most of all, by this new trumpet-love. Fred Walker's old rotary-change instrument was joined a year or so later by another pre-war narrow-bore model, from Harry Strauss Junior. But there were other wonderful junkshops all around Southend and in one, a couple of years later, I found my first short cornet too – a sweet, small instrument, nestling in its handmade darkwood brass band case. I knew instantly I wanted this instrument very much indeed; Bix Beiderbecke, Ruby Braff and Wild Bill Davison – three names I revered – played cornets as opposed to trumpets and the instrument had a proud jazz heritage. Derek Wood sensed my problem and offered me half a crown an hour to work in his garden. I earned a crisp ten shilling note – but not enough for the cornet! So, into a sack went most of what was left of my boyhood possessions – an airgun and airpistol, a bow and arrows, a fishing rod, an old military drum from the remains of my home-made drum kit along with anything else that I could sacrifice – and we drove into town and up to Leigh. Given the situation it's surprising I didn't ask Ena to throw our car into the deal. 'My God,' said the shopkeeper, sensing an invasion as we made our clamorous entrance, and slipped a pill into his mouth.

'I'm an aspirin addict,' he explained to Ena, further sullying the already suspect image of jazz.

'I really would love to have that cornet,' I began. 'And I've got a few things I could perhaps part-exchange as well as this ten shillings.' I dipped into the sack, hurling all my possessions including football boots, a recorder, a ukelele, an old guitar into a heap on the shop floor. After three or four minutes of watching the pile grow ever higher, the shopkeeper gave in.

'Oh, go on then! Just take the bloody thing!'

And home we drove! Soon I began consciously playing on what trumpet teachers call a 'non-central embouchure' – in other words, from the side of my mouth. Several of my role-models: Ruby Braff, Wild Bill Davison and Bruce Turner (albeit on alto saxophone) played from the side. So, I discovered later, did the veteran British trumpeter Nat Gonella. So why shouldn't I? The mouthpiece felt comfortable off centre and I thought it might mark me out as worth a second look.

And as this would never be more than a hobby, what was there to lose in any case?

In 1961 I heard my first jazz concerts at Southend Pier's Sun Deck Theatre. These were the years of the British 'trad boom' when premier-league traditional jazz musicians were as famous as popstars and for me the most dynamic, technically efficient and entertaining band of the boom was Kenny Ball and his Jazzmen. Following Kenny at a respectful distance on the pier train after his concert, then pursuing him up Pier Hill, I plucked up courage and knocked on his limousine window as he was about to drive off. Obligingly he stopped and wound the window down.

'Excuse me, Mr Ball,' I said. 'The concert was marvellous! And could you please tell me the trumpet-valve fingerings for top A B and C?' Kenny cocked his head and thought for a moment. 'One and two, middle, then open! OK?' And with a wave he sped away. I had had my first trumpet lesson from Britain's premier star.

My favourite concert, though, was by Bruce Turner's Jump Band. Divorced stylistically from the traditional jazz boom then sweeping Britain, the Jump Band had no mass following and played to about ten people in the Sun Deck Theatre. As usual, I made efforts to travel back in the same coach as the band on the pier train and, spying the leader half way up Pier Hill, ran up with an autograph book.

'Would you mind signing this, Mr Turner?'

'Sure Dad, sure Dad!' (It should be explained that Bruce Turner not only said almost everything twice but also called everyone 'Dad', including his daughters!).

'Hold these!' He handed me a clutch of ice-cream cornets and signed. It was a beautiful sunny evening, and the swing music I'd heard was ringing in my ears. 'You sound as if you like Pee Wee Russell.'

'Sure Dad, sure Dad! Love Pee Wee! Great! Great!'

Playing jazz with a real band seemed, at that point, an

Bruce Turner

impossible dream. But one day, in school assembly, a whisper came along the row. Tomorrow night, a real jazz band would play in a barn, not many miles away from Paglesham. I'd heard the name too: Dave Mills and his New Orleans Jazzmen. Mills – who later joined the Temperance Seven, then became a radio-presenter in Saudi Arabia – had been youth mayor of South-end but was now making up for this virtuous public debut by leading a jazz band from behind his drums. So, on Saturday night, I took my trumpet and found my destination. The barn, with hay stacked in its corners, was crowded with admiring listeners and the band blew the kind of committed traditional jazz I'd only heard on record. Among its sidemen were a young star of the traditional boom, trumpeter John 'Kid' Shillito, and bassist Stan Leader, a veteran of Cy Laurie's groups.

I asked if I might sit in. 'You can lead the band', said generous John, stepping to one side to leave me to it. For the next few intoxicating minutes, in Nat Gonella's down-to-earth phrase, I 'blew my head off' and while what I played had nothing to do with the cultivated New Orleans style of Dave's band, a happy and generous crowd, out for a good time, gave me a rousing hand. The immediate problem was that by the end of my number the excitement of the moment had combined with an unexpected left-field element: waves of the strongest perfume I'd ever smelt, wafting from an enthusiastic lady at stage-side! The chemistry of this combination made me certain I was going to be very ill indeed.

'Come on!' said John Shillito, 'that was fine! Play another one!'

'Later maybe,' I spluttered and ran outside until the nausea had passed.

In 1961, largely at John Fairweather's instigation, I auditioned in London for the National Youth Orchestra in the presence of one of the orchestra's principals, the formidable and eminent Dame Ruth Railton. Dame Ruth listened to my carefully prepared solo with moderate interest but couldn't understand why most of what I was doing, including reading a simple audition passage, sounded so wheezily non-enthusiastic. To my alarm she came behind me at close of play, and firmly grasped what you might call my upper bronchial areas, one in each triumphant hand.

'Well really!' she protested to bemused Ena, who was watching nearby. 'I can't understand what's wrong. The boy has a *lovely* pair of chests!'

I failed the audition but the thrill of the day had already gone by: a trip to London's most famous jazz record shop, Dobell's.

Imagine the magic: a bright, golden London morning; traversing old Cambridge Circus through taxis, buses and traffic and down Charing Cross Road, rich in music shops, to number 77 on the right hand side. This was the retail outlet started by Doug Dobell with a box of second-hand 78s back in the late 1940s and now, without question, the greatest jazz record shop in the country. You went through the glass-panelled door lined with posters for concerts, pub gigs, and jazz clubs and then, on the right, stood the long counter, behind which towered the imposing figure of Don Solash, Dobell's son-in-law. Tony Middleton – shorter, more gregarious and more approachable – and others moved efficiently about, serving customers who formed a line from the door. Above the wooden browser-boxes, LP covers created colourful images along the walls. Beyond the counter were private listening booths, each with its own door, turntable, heavy pick-up and speaker. And beyond these, through a poster-lined glass-panelled door, Doug Dobell could be seen at work at his desk.

Best of all perhaps, though, was to do what I did that day – turn left halfway down the shop and descend a winding shadowy staircase to the near-legendary second-hand record department of John Kendall – a musical university to the 1950s generation of jazz graduates-to-be. John, as usual, was behind the counter, a shot of whisky not far away. And the music on the speakers, as I found out through years of visits, would always be of five star quality: Duke Ellington, Louis Armstrong, Billie Holiday and their peers. Sometimes, descending the staircase brought you face to face with a jazz legend, yarning and enjoying John's company. On one occasion I found tenorist Ben Webster in full conversational flow, legs outstretched on a short hard chair.

To begin with, I was as overwhelmed by the sight of John as by that of the rest of Dobell's cast of characters. But, having digested the delights of his cellar and re-mounted the stairs, I was about to leave when music from the shop's speakers hit me as hard as any music had done so far. It was Billie Holiday singing 'Carelessly' with Cootie Williams' passionate plunger-muted sixteen bars capping the closing chorus. Running back down the stairs, I approached John, 'What are they playing, please?'

'The new Billie Holiday,' he said. 'You'll have to buy it upstairs.'

Which I did, aware that the entire Dobell's staff – no doubt including John – would have preferred not to have to take this marvellous music off the turntable. But the deal was sealed. And I left with the latest 'Giant Jazz Gallery' LP masterpiece – Billie Holiday's 'This is My Last Affair' – safe in its carrier-bag, hallmarked with the legendary slogan 'Every true jazz fan is born within the sound of Dobell's'!

Over the years, Dobell's remained first-stop for jazz records in London. Not far away, waiting in the wings were Ray's Jazz Shop in Shaftesbury Avenue and the tiny shop in New Row belonging to James Asman. But no other shop back then had quite the hipness of Dobell's inner-sanctum. As time passed John Kendall came to know me a little and would hiss, 'There's a new box there – just in!'

John's dry sense of humour came to the fore one day when elderly Ian Nichols, an aristocratic jazz connoisseur, brought his equally up-market and elderly wife, Jean, to John's basement to wait while he browsed the boxes. Possibly feeling neglected, Jean opened the conversational batting with a P.G. Woodhouse motif, 'I'm finding more and more,' she observed to anyone who might be listening, 'how terribly hard it is to get good staff these days.'

John glanced across from his conversation and whisky glass. 'Same trouble in here, love!' he nodded.

It was sad when, after many years, declining fortunes compelled Dobell to sack his longtime employee, and for a few years the evacuee set up shop for himself in a hideaway near to Seven Dials. More often, however, he was to be found drinking with friends in The Two Brewers nearby. Doug Dobell himself collapsed and died at the Nice Jazz Festival a few years later. Neither the shop, nor jazz in London would ever be quite the same again.

Jazz became my twenty-four-hours-a-day passion. There was no shortage of inspiration; the jazz gods still walked the earth and in 1962 Louis Armstrong came to Southend. Flanked by his All Stars, he filled the Odeon Cinema with a great gold wave of sound that enveloped the audience like sunshine. Armstrong and his right-hand man Trummy Young played like kings and clowned irresistibly, slapping each other's palms after each glorious solo. Afterwards there was nothing to do but catch the country bus as far as it went and then walk the remaining three miles home savouring the sounds of the greatest jazz music, as it rang in our heads and echoed across the flat country fields.

Over the next few years, more jazz stars came to Southend including Ella Fitzgerald with Oscar Peterson and the Coleman Hawkins-Roy Eldridge Quintet. Hawkins, like an old bearded god, spilled out great metallic phrases from his tenor, while Eldridge played cautiously within himself, as he often did on first house, before his lip loosened up for stratospheric trumpet gymnastics later. Ella, at the peak of her mature form, carolled a version of 'In a Mellotone' that stays clearly in my mind. Other visitors included Count Basie and his orchestra with Jimmy Rushing, Sarah Vaughan and her trio (the rapt silence as she made her perfect pinpoint way through the ballad 'Misty' was unforgettable) and Woody Herman. Duke Ellington at the newly opened Cliffs Pavilion – with Johnny Hodges, Harry Carney and all the centrepieces of his orchestra intact – was simply the most elegant man I have ever seen.

At Southend High School I acquired the nickname of Digby from a posh fellow pupil in a school queue and the name was to remain with me in my professional life. Once I'd made it into the sixth form the work-pace hotted up considerably but every Friday came a treasured oasis of pleasure time. Carrying my school briefcase – fattened by records purchased from the monosyllabic Strauss – I would head for a seat overlooking the seafront to devour the weekly contents of *Melody Maker* and contemplate the darkening estuary waters and glowing orange lights of Kent beyond, as I sat waiting for the doors to open at the Studio Jazz Club.

In the club, around nine-thirty, Kenny Baxter's Southend Modern Jazz Quintet (SMJQ) played all the latest, most hip music. The front-line partners were Kenny on tenor saxophone and the young trumpeter, Vic Wood, who had won the *Daily Mail*'s brass band competition at the age of seven against adult players – in order to ensure an objective musical decision the finalists had played behind a curtain, and Vic had won anyhow! Kenny regularly invited all the top London tenorists, from Jimmy Skidmore and Kathy Stobart to Don Rendell, to join him at Studio Jazz.

One Friday night in 1963, a quartet of jazz stormtroopers came to the club unheralded: Dave Tomlin, soprano; Jack Bruce, bass; drummer Jon Hiseman and, on piano, the tragic Mike Taylor who would later commit suicide by walking into the sea at Southend. They played a thunderously challenging set of near-free Coltrane music; no comforting standards, no reference to the cosy bebop jazz heritage – nothing, in fact, to smooth their audience's collective brow. This music all but caused fights amongst its outraged listeners and was my introduction to the challenging matter of keeping up with changing musical times.

By this time I had formed a quartet, including my old friend Dirk Wood on piano and the club agreed to let us play during intermissions. We quickly got used to the discouraging sight of fans in their dozens filing out in the direction of the Queens' Hotel up the road (Studio Jazz was unlicensed) while we nervously took over the stand.

On another evening, the Studio was enlivened by the appearance of altoist Joe Harriott, his friend the pianist Haig Joyce and, direct from the legendary Studio 51 Jazz Club in New Compton Street, Soho, compère, commentator and jazz institution Bix Curtis. This night there was a singer with our band – tall, with raven black hair and an hourglass figure – making her winsome way through 'Whisper Not' in Anita O'Day style. Bix stood in front of her to show his appreciation and introduce himself in his typical, outrageously macho and exuberant fashion, by making as if to drop his trousers!

Bix's contribution to British jazz had been extensive. He took most of the blame and little of the credit for encouraging, in defiance of union rules, American stars like Sidney Bechet and Coleman Hawkins onto British stages and over the years which followed he became a close friend.

At this time I still also played the clarinet but had decided – for the sake of volume – to use an alto-saxophone reed in its mouthpiece. This gave me a big sound but didn't deter the audience from going off to the pub as usual, come intermission time! MC Barry Woodie, however, pointed out to drummer Dave Mills that I might be the man to fill a vacant clarinet chair in his New Orleans Jazzmen. So, in 1962-3 I played for the first time in a real traditional jazz band – several gigs with Dave's band – but later was quite rightly dropped from the group for playing in too 'modern' a style. It may also have been my commitment to study for A-levels that gave the leader a perfectly reasonable chance to stabilise his stylistic output. But nothing mattered! Jazz was already a perfectly good reason for living and there was a lot of living to do.

2.

further down the brass track

In 1964 I left school and began work as a solicitor's clerk (which I hated) before moving to a job in Southend Library. There was no question of making music professionally. I'd failed music 'O' level and everyone in my family said, 'you must get a job – that's life!' Life as a librarian seemed agreeable enough: the profession seemed humanitarian, vaguely artistic and devoid of pressure. And a bonus – my first real girlfriend, Barbara Rudling, was working there too.

One morning, in spring 1965, I took my trumpet from its case after a layoff of several months and, when I blew, a huge effortlessly fat note sprang immediately from the bell. This was a transformation from the limited sounds of one year before, in the wake of which – obsessed with the business of a first real romance – I'd left off playing at all. My new sound turned my head like vintage wine. Somewhere during my layoff for love an embouchure had set, and this was a good one.

From that moment, my trumpet and I were inseparable. 'It's time for lessons,' I thought. 'There's something here worth polishing.' So, soon after, I began studies with E.M. 'Bert' Collier, one-time lead trumpeter for Joe Loss. Bert was the perfect instructor, gently correcting faults and full of encouragement. 'You're playing the trumpet very well, Dick! And if you continue playing as you are now, you will be the finest trumpet player in the country!' Each Sunday morning I came home from my lesson glowing with musical hopes planted by my teacher and ready to play better than ever.

As I got to know Bert, he instructed me in other aspects of music too, 'When you play the trumpet Dick, never listen to anyone but the other musicians. *Theirs* is the opinion you should look out for.' He was similarly wise in the business of playing with assurance. 'Keep your confidence here, Dick,' my teacher would say, patting his stomach and smiling quietly. 'But never,' – the same hand to his lips now – 'never, let it come out here!'

In later years Bert moved to Guildford to live with his son and for a while we lost touch. Then, in 1983, I received the sad news of his death. The funeral service was held in Guildford Cathedral and, mid-way through, the minister announced, 'Now Digby Fairweather will play the trumpet.' Standing alone in a pew, I played 'Swing Low Sweet Chariot' as well as I could for my old friend and teacher.

By the mid-1960s, I was aware that there are few feelings greater than being in total control of a musical instrument while playing the music you love. And at this happy time, I felt my trumpet playing could charm the birds from the trees. From 1965, I played regularly with the local Mel Lewis dance band and sometimes we were booked to play in London, notably at the Connaught Hotel in Park Lane to a huge crowd with a fully-uniformed master of ceremonies. From the back of the room the MC heard me play and walked to the stand to tug the trouser leg of my uniform. 'I'll say one thing for you, young whippersnapper,' he pronounced, 'you certainly can play that trumpet of yours!' I felt proud to be praised by such a tough critic in stylish Mayfair.

In 1965 I often sat in with visiting jazz stars in Southend too. Monty Sunshine allowed me several tunes. And only once was a request refused: by Ken Colyer: 'We don't have sitters-in, man!' he explained bluntly and was quite right to do so. In retrospect I feel fortunate that so many of Britain's traditional jazz fraternity were prepared to bend rules on a youngster's behalf.

Many Thursday nights that year I sat in at Southend Rhythm Club too. Visiting stars included Kathy Stobart and her husband Bert Courtley (a wildly under-rated and tragedy-bound trumpeter), Art Ellefson, Les Condon, and in particular Don Rendell who, in the course of one evening, gave me more encouragement than any other professional musician had up to then. I rediscovered this inbuilt gentility when Bix Curtis invited my intermission troupe to back Don and his friend, Jimmy Skidmore, for an evening. We knew none of their tunes and the proceedings limped along amid wrong chord-changes, breakdowns, and excursions into the musical dark. I was distraught for the guests and stammering out apologies when Don stopped me.

'Dig,' he said gently, 'it's fine. Jimmy and I had a lot of fun. It's just a shame we couldn't play a few more of our favourites for everyone but no matter!'

Tenorist Jimmy Skidmore was one of the greatest characters British jazz ever knew. 'Allo darlin',' was his regular greeting, usually followed rapidly by, 'Kiss yer bum later,' the phrase he had whispered in Louis Armstrong's ear – much to Louis' astonished delight – at an otherwise reverential first meeting in the dressing room with Humphrey Lyttelton's band with which Jimmy worked back in 1956.

Jimmy, as Humph remembers in his book *Second Chorus,* was vocationally irreverent: a broad tusky grin on offer to the world, usually in the wake of his own irrepressibility. On one occasion Humph was bemused to hear his audience breaking into laughter in the middle of a dramatic trumpet solo and stepped back to discover that Jimmy's false teeth were balanced on the mouthpiece of his tenor saxophone! At another concert, while announcing a new number, Humph found himself unexpectedly assailed from behind as Jimmy grasped a generous proportion of his leader's trouser seat.

'I'm touching the governor's bum!' he explained to the delighted audience.

One thing that surprised me at this time was how divorced members of the jazz community were from the burgeoning pop music scene that I continued to be fascinated with. One evening in 1966, a misguided visitor asked Jimmy if he knew 'Elusive Butterfly', then a hit for the folk-style singer Bob Lind.

'What's that, darlin'?' asked Jimmy. 'Elusive whatsit? No – don't know that one – sorry!'

'Fuck off nicely, then,' he added.

One evening in 1965, Jimmy's superb set had been watched by a young, enthralled saxophonist, carrying her alto case. Afterwards she timidly approached the master to ask if he had any tips for a young student of the saxophone.

'Certainly, ducks!' said Jimmy. 'Blow nice and hard. And keep your arse closed!'

I joined Jimmy and Bix Curtis in 1965 to play my first real professional jazz concert in the unlikely surroundings of Lewes Prison in Sussex, with piano, bass, drums and a sultry singer who wore dark glasses throughout her set and valiantly braved the audible expressions of delight from an audience short of female company. The reception was ecstatic, and afterwards we went to tea in a nearby café, the singer still in her dark glasses.

'Come on, darlin',' said Jimmy, 'Show us yer minces! [pies = eyes] That's nice, love. Kiss yer bum!'

After tea we drove to a famous jazz venue, the Fox and Hounds at Haywards Heath where, four years later, I would meet Alex Welsh and his band for the first time. That night, the resident Fourteen Foot Band was joined by pianist Lennie Felix and I was encouraged to sit in for a tune or two. If there was a happier young man in Britain that night as we drove home (Bix accelerating round corners while producing convincing impressions of a police siren in pursuit) I'd like to have met him.

There was also a blues club in Southend at the time and, one night, I found myself playing with Champion Jack

Jimmy Skidmore

Dupree, a former boxer. Jack interspersed his authentic blues singing and rolling boogie piano with well-rehearsed gags, punctuated with a gold-toothed smile. 'As Shakespeare said....' he would begin, eyebrows rising and falling with the speed of windscreen wipers, 'why should a young girl never marry a football player?'

Then a well-timed pause before the punchline: 'because he always dribble before he shoot!'

He had a fund of wonderful and highly risqué blues, including the wonderful 'Dr Dupree Blues'.

'Calling Dr Dupree, he's the best surgery man in town.
He can operate on a woman and she don't even have to lay down!'

Behind his goodtime image, though, Jack was a smooth and efficient businessman who regularly, so it was said, ran shopping-trips from his Sheffield council house in a gold plated Rolls Royce. He was very kind to me on our first meeting, 'I was at the Reno Club with Count Basie and all those cats,' he told me, 'and I'm tellin' you: you're as good as any of those trumpet-playin' guys down there!'

Later on, in the early 1970s, I played with Jack again and the last time I saw him was just before he died, at the Burnley Blues Festival around 1992. Older and sadder, he sang a blues titled 'I Wish I'd Played With the Beatles'.

In the summer of 1966 I decided it was time to take London's jazz scene by storm. I was sure I was playing brilliantly, so – within a week in town – I would be able to sit in everywhere, make my mark, and emerge as Britain's newest trumpet star! I packed a bag and checked in at the Bloomsbury Hotel in the West End.

My only firm invitation was from Jimmy Skidmore. 'Sit in with me any time you want, darlin'!' he had said. So I made my way to the Plough at Stockwell to stand self-consciously amid the crowd, trumpet-case semi-hidden. Harry Stoneham was playing piano, Jimmy Collins played alto with a grace comparable to Benny Carter's and Jimmy himself poured out choruses of fluent tenor, between relaxing at his chosen playing point next to the ladies' lavatory. 'Save us a seat, ducks!' he would remind those going in, while those on the way out were greeted with: 'Could you hear us out here, ducks? That's nice! We could hear you in there too!'

Thanks to Jimmy, I managed to sit in for a couple of nervous numbers and next night, having studied the columns of *Melody Maker*, made my way to the 100 Club where Eric Silk's Southern Jazz Band was playing. Eric was rightly firm, 'Sorry Digby, no sitters-in!'

'Tread softly, for you tread on my dreams,' floated through my mind but, undeterred, I found a pub where trumpeter Fred Shaw led a dixieland band. Fred could hold a top C while scratching his head or lifting a pint glass, and regularly did. I asked to sit in and seemed to make a mildly favourable impression although I had nothing like Fred's remarkable range. 'And he's only playing in a pub?' I wondered to myself. Plainly this was the big city!

But playing in a pub wasn't exactly what I'd had in mind – even though it was a start. So the next night I went to a club proper – in a room *above* a pub! Due to play was altoist Dudu Pukwana, newly arrived from South Africa, and there he was, talking earnestly with colleagues around the piano. Shamelessly, I approached them and asked if sitting in might be allowed. Dudu looked me up and down.

'Would you mind waiting outside, with the rest of our audience?' he asked. It was unanswerably the right response but I was crushed and made my way back to Fred Shaw's band for a couple more tunes before packing and heading home to Paglesham. London wasn't ready for me yet.

That same year, in Southend, I had a first try at leading a dixieland band of my own. This involved assembling a few friendly musicians for rehearsals; we even played one job. But for now that had to be it – I was due to attend Library College from September 1966. This involved an interview at London's Northwest Polytechnic.

'Which authors have you read?' I was asked.

I'd spent the previous evening thumbing through a friend's collection of *Playboy* magazines, and no doubt short of mental energy as a result, could think of only one recent book: Miss Read's delightful but innocuous *Thrush Green*. 'Oh,' said my interrogators and failed me flat. In the next few weeks, I boned up on Steinbeck, Hemingway and their contemporaries and was accepted at Ealing Technical College.

From 1966-8 I studied librarianship and took the retrograde step of trying to play the trumpet from the centre of my mouth, which sent me dishearteningly back to the beginning for four long years. The only showbusiness distinction of my college years was that a fellow student was Freddie Mercury!

After college, I went back to work in the library, broadened my experience of jazz and carried on playing around Southend, to very mixed effect. For the first of several periods in my playing career, people were asking themselves what had happened. A year or two previously, I had been playing with ease. Now I was audibly wrestling with my new central embouchure. Nevertheless, one Sunday afternoon, as I was walking from a local jam session, a young man introduced himself. 'I'm Trevor Taylor,' he said. 'What are you doing with all that old-style junk? Come and play with me sometime and try something new! There's a rehearsal hall I've fixed up – drop in any time!'

Trevor was a highly-skilled drummer who also went on to run FMR Music and to publish *Avant* magazine. His area of operations was free jazz and he was already a postmodernist by conviction, a young innovator who knew and understood the music of Joe Zawinul, Mike Gibbs and their contemporaries and talked enthusiastically of the work of new British players like John Taylor, Henry Lowther and Harry Beckett as well as true revolutionaries such as guitarist Derek Bailey.

For months I frequented Trevor's open-house studio: really a big shed down an alley. He was the first person to show me a synthesizer; it looked then like a cross between a small telephone exchange and a draughts board and challenged the user to produce any sound at all. Through Trevor I learned that you could write a score in non-traditional notation – or even play a picture, sketched on a piece of paper! And one evening the eminent avant-garde bassist Barry Guy came to the studio, sharing his expertise in this new music.

Trevor wrote a big abstract piece for around forty players and to record it took an ensemble to London, combining string players from the local college (no interest in jazz) with local heroes and trumpeter Harry Beckett. Then he multi-tracked the recording three times more, a semitone apart each time! The result must have sounded like Judgment Day but I remember clearly one beautiful note from Harry hanging above the landscape of sound like a flash of dawn light in a grey sky.

One day Trevor composed an almost impossibly obscure atonal ballad. Its premier, on which I played, began before a relatively full audience in the upper room of a Southend pub. When I opened my eyes at the end of a long solo, the last two members of our audience were hurrying out in search of something a bit less demanding!

Trevor pitched me into playing technically challenging music and encouraged me to take lessons from Harry Beckett, at that time a polltopper in *Melody Maker*. Harry did his best to teach me for weeks in Stoke Newington and I learned a lot about contemporary jazz. He endured with fortitude the fact that his new pupil seldom, if ever, practised the exercises patiently written out for him. ('Can you play them? OK then ... that's fine!') but I was, in fact, far more interested in the window on the jazz scene that our meetings afforded. One afternoon I noticed that my teacher seemed pre-occupied and after a while asked if everything was alright.

'Well,' said Harry, after a pause. 'My son was knocked over by a car this morning and he's in hospital just now, seriously injured.'

'Why,' I asked, dismayed, 'didn't you ring and cancel?'

'Well, you'd made all the arrangements to come after all. It's a long way. So how could I let you down!'

Throughout the time I was experimenting with Trevor Taylor and new music, I continued to play with the Mel Lewis Band. By the mid-1960s a fine Lee Konitz-influenced alto player, Jim Livesey, had joined the group and he later asked me to join his quintet. We rehearsed complex small charts in multiple time-signatures with forays into free improvisation, receiving a mixed reaction when we played at the Red Lion at Margaretting.

Pianist Derek Wood was now living in East London and after closing time I would sleep on his floor for three or four hours before making my way by train to Southend to join the Mobile Library at 8.45 am. No chance of a proper breakfast of course, so each morning I would drop into a workmen's café opposite the bus garage (where the Mobile Library was parked off-duty) and order the nearest thing to breakfast they had available on the menu – ravioli and ice-cream!

Spotting my enthusiasm for the vocation of full-time musician, Trevor Taylor had warned me, 'Don't leave it too late, Dig,' and he was absolutely right. Devoted to music but locked into a nine-to-five job, I was building a double life for myself: double standards, dual beliefs.

Alex Welsh

In 1969, after hearing Alex Welsh's band on record for years, I heard them live at the Fox and Hounds, Haywards Heath. That night was to focus my way of thinking about jazz for a quarter of a century. Diminutive, circular-faced, cornetist Alex led his players casually onto the stand and they opened with Kenny Graham's arrangement of 'Opus One'. The sound of four melded tones from four burnished bells hit me in harmony and I knew immediately that this was the best band in Britain! Afterwards I joined one of the after-hours parties the Welsh band relished, hosted by landlord Chris Worrell. As his guests sat around, a projector was brought in and Laurel and Hardy's 'County Hospital,' was shown to roars of laughter. Alex and Fred played more duets and much drink was taken.

During the party I asked Alex silly standard questions: why a cornet rather than a trumpet, which mouthpiece he used and much more and he took time to talk, and to answer my questions, amid the revelry. It may well have been that night that Alex's drummer, Lennie Hastings, went to bed in the small hours leaving his infamous toupee at the bedside. Its removal transformed Lennie from a reasonably handsome man into something rather more aged and bedraggled. When a young waitress delivered a tray of tea to his bedroom next morning, Lennie rose from the sheet depths like some prematurely-aged cadavre. The tray of tea flew into the air.

I was now sure I loved dixieland jazz more than any other but continued broadening my jazz education nevertheless. Trawling through the marvellous old *Decca Book of Jazz*, I read Tony Hall's essay, 'Nice Work If You Can Get It', on Britain's bebop beginnings with the Club Eleven and found a new pre-occupation. Perhaps there might be a book to be researched from those few passionate years? So I made appointments with the staff at *Melody Maker*, including dear Max Jones, who allowed me full access to make longhand notes from files at their premises – at this point located in south London and forbiddingly surrounded by barbed wire.

I also began interviews – with Kathy Stobart and Ronnie Scott – for the purpose of my planned book. Kathy talked for hours with me at her Upper Norwood home and it was only when pushing the button on my cassette recorder to play back our conversation on the way home that I learnt – the hard way – the interviewer's first rule: check your battery-levels! The whole conversation had been recorded on a failing set of batteries and when I played it back at full speed on new ones, Kathy and I sounded like Minnie and Micky Mouse on helium.

Still I persevered. Tony Hall's 'Nice Work' essay had turned the spotlight on Denis Rose, trumpeter, pianist and guru to Britain's modern jazz generation. So, while interviewing Ronnie Scott one evening at Frith Street, I asked him if Denis was still around. 'He's in here most nights,' said Ronnie adding that his old tutor was also working at the Affair Club nearby in Denman Street. So I called the club and spoke, in wonder, to a man who claimed he was Denis Rose, founder of Britain's bebop revolution.

A few nights later, wearing a fading flower-power outfit with bright-pink bell-bottom trousers, I made my way to the Affair Club, armed with tape-recorder and (fresh) batteries! This was poor choice of dress code as the Affair turned out to be a gay club and several swarthy men surrounded me hoping for a piece of the action and suggesting explicitly where and how it might be found. 'No, no!' I spluttered, 'I'm here for the piano player.'

'Who's a lucky boy then?' one of my assailants nodded as he and his friends finally gave up on me.

At the piano, Denis was playing simple, pleasant duets with bass-trumpeter Dave Burns. Afterwards I introduced myself to my hero who suggested we go to Ronnie's for a while. 'He's a good friend,' said Denis. 'I make up tapes of funny shows for him.' So we walked the few blocks to Frith Street where Rose talked to friends, including Tony Crombie stylishly dressed in leather cowboy waistcoat and stetson.

Later, Denis suggested we might take a cab up to the council flat in Highgate where he lived with his wife. And there we talked all night. He remembered working for the legendary West End gangster, Jack Spot, in clubs with gay entertainers, as well as the whole bebop revolution and the Club Eleven, twenty years previously. He was rightly proud of an interview with Peter Clayton, broadcast on 'Jazznotes' not long before, and also played the big band tapes (mentioned in Tony Hall's essay) that he had written and recorded at home, playing

every instrument. All night my recorder rolled in a conversation impeded only by the young interviewer's elementary
errors: cutting across answers with more questions, leaving
insufficient time for his interviewee to think, and altogether
rolling at speed down an over-keen road. Somewhere along
the way I asked my new acquaintance: 'How do you feel
about bebop these days?'

'I don't believe in it any more,' said Denis simply. 'Not the
way you do.'

The bebop revolution had been no more than twenty years
before but to both of us, apparently, it seemed like another
world. I left his flat to make for the milk train as the dawn
was coming up and he was heading for bed. I never met Denis
again, sadly, but my article on the meeting was published in
Melody Maker and tapes of this early, amateurish attempt at
an interview are filed at the National Sound Archive Jazz
Division at Kings Cross, London.

By 1970, I'd spent four years trying to play trumpet as others
play it, with a dead central embouchure. The sound I produced was dead in more ways than one. It was poor and harsh
and what I could play was governed entirely by my instrument, not by musical thoughts in my head. So, one evening, I
placed the mouthpiece back at the side of my mouth and felt
the notes roll out like honey. I could play the trumpet again!
Within days people were looking up in pleased surprise. The
feeling of joyous liberation was beyond words, like letting all
your feelings out after bottling them up for years.

Around this time too, I changed to cornet full-time. In
Lewington's – London's long-established musical instrument
centre at Cambridge Circus – I discovered the sweet-toned
Yamaha long-model (a recent arrival in Britain) and my course
with this instrument was set for life.

The dixieland persuasions of the music I began playing at
this time didn't please all my former colleagues but, for me, it
felt right. It could be only a question of time before I formed
a band to play this carefree music. In the meantime, there

were jazz sessions at the Red Lion, Margaretting: Nevil
Skrimshire on guitar, myself on cornet, John Mole on bass
and, on one occasion, altoist Bruce Turner who agreed
to come for six or seven pounds – a much lower fee than he
deserved.

Bruce was regularly to be found in the midst of strange situations and this night at the Red Lion was one of them. One
half-hour before the session was due to begin, a man who
looked exactly like Bruce Turner walked into the wrong bar
at the Red Lion carrying a case. I followed him in.

'Mr Bruce Turner?'

'Not me, not me!'

'But surely you're here to play for us?'

'Not me, not me. Don't play, don't play!'

And out he went. Half an hour later Bruce walked in and
played like an angel!

At half time, I asked, 'Would you like a drink, Bruce?'

'No dad, no dad! Wouldn't mind a box of chocolates
though!' The barlady went and found one for him.

American musicians visited the Red Lion too. One was my
role model Dick Sudhalter, then living in London and soon to
author the biography of Bix Beiderbecke, *Bix, Man and
Legend*. Dick played the cornet exquisitely in the style of
Bobby Hackett and knew more tunes than any musician I'd
met up to then. Another American visitor was the pianist Joe
Albany who had recorded with Charlie Parker and other
bebop giants. Joe had taken up temporary residence in
Britain with critic-entrepreneur Tony Williams and he made
his British debut at the Red Lion with Jim Livesey, myself,
John Mole and drummer Dave Meakin. This was a small his-
toric moment in British jazz terms and it got into the jazz
press too.

At this point, I began to reconsider the dreamlike possibility
of working in London! Should I perhaps try for a job or two
in one of the many dixieland pubs on the Essex side of
London? One night, taking courage and telephone in hand

I rang the Cauliflower in Ilford, and asked to speak to 'the guv'nor'.

'I'm him,' said the answering voice. 'Back in a minute!' and the phone was laid down. While I was waiting for it to be picked up again, the sound of phenomenal bebop trumpeting rang down the wires: obviously this man was a record collector and knew his jazz. So perhaps he might be on my side?

'That's a wonderful record you're playing!' I said when the voice came back to the phone. 'Is it Clifford Brown?'

'No mate,' said my supposed employer-to-be. 'That's Gerry Salisbury. He's playing here in the public bar.'

'Well, nice to talk to you!' I said, and hung up. This was London! Multi-instrumentalist Gerry Salisbury would in future years become a good friend and years later he played bass in my small group, Fairweather Friends.

I was now travelling to gigs further afield and getting back late to Stannetts. This late return was also to do with my girlfriend at the time who had also worked on the mobile library. Together we had watched the moon-landing on television and began celebrating the event soon after, frequently into the small hours. My amoreuse had a boyfriend already but charitably slipped me into spare hours and, somewhere between three and four in the morning, I would emerge from her flat pleasurably exhausted, find a cab and search frantically for a snatch of sleep at Stannetts before getting up for work. Although there were other serious girlfriends, I was in all personal respects a strange young man. For the years to come, every natural instinct – from marriage to fatherhood – was deliberately subjugated to the cause of jazz.

In short, I was married to my cornet and the time seemed right to form a band of my own. The music that I'd come back to time and again was dixieland. Everyone in my immediate circle dismissively called such music 'trad' and implied that playing it was a simple exercise unworthy of consideration by 'serious' modern musicians. Assembling sympathetic musicians around Essex was none too easy either but a search located clarinettist Ollie Dow, pianist Bunny Courtenay, trombonist Jeff Goodman (brother of British bop drummer Benny Goodman) and the young drummer, Alan Clarke, who'd played with me in a very early try at a dixieland band in 1965. So what should we call the group? 'How about Dig's Half Dozen?' suggested Ollie Dow. Agreed!

The Half Dozen made its debut at the Red Lion, Margaretting, in 1970 and quickly built a local following. Landlord Gordon Worthy loved the group and, while not actually going so far as to *pay* us, agreed to find the fees for famous visitors. As a result, guests who came to play with us over the next year or so included trumpeter Ray Crane, trombonist John Picard and Jimmy Skidmore. We also found a venue in a Southend seafront pub and opened with special guest Bruce Turner.

But I had my eye on bigger venues than Southend pubs. Excusing myself from mobile library duties to find nearby phone-boxes I repeatedly badgered Roger Horton, the famous proprietor of London's home of traditional jazz, the 100 Club.

'Digby,' said Roger, early in 1971, 'I'm *sure* you have a good band. But I never use unknown talent. Ever!'

'Please Mr Horton. We won't let you down. After all, my trombonist's brother was Benny Goodman!'

Finally, under the pressure of my non-stop calls, Roger gave in. 'OK Digby. I'll put you on as second group on Saturday, June 23rd.'

'Who will we be supporting?' I asked.

'Let me see now,' said Roger consulting his schedule. 'Oh yes, it's Alex Welsh!'

Our little band was to play at the legendary 100 Club!

The Half Dozen rehearsed to exhaustion. I was in a fever of excitement, praying that we would be good enough. When we arrived at the club it was half-full already: Alex was a sure Saturday night draw. Our little group set up bravely on the stage, and at eight o'clock launched into our signature-song 'Sleepy Time Gal'. From the first note I knew we were in with more than a chance. Amid the echoing acoustics of the club and generous PA provision the band sounded as good as ever it could. Every soloist rose to the occasion and I played as hard as I knew how. When we left the stand five or six numbers later, Alex was there to meet me at the bar, hand outstretched in greeting.

'Remember me?' he said. Remember Alex? Of course I did, but how or why on earth did he remember me?

'I do!' he confirmed. 'We had an interesting conversation at the Fox and Hounds. And let me tell you something, lad! Not only are you a *great* trumpet player, but this is the finest new band I've ever played opposite. Congratulations!' I was speechless. After this generous man took the stand, he said exactly the same thing to his audience and once again we were treated to warm applause. It was one of the happiest nights of my young life. Now, for sure, the only way was up!

1971, however, brought the saddest news of my life so far. On 6th July I was at Stannetts watching the television evening news and it began with a picture of Louis Armstrong. The greatest jazz trumpeter had died. As the evening lengthened I took my horn down to the deserted kitchen and – with a straight-mute set in its bell – looked up at the smiling poster of Armstrong while I played him a tearful blues. I wasn't the only one who was devastated. Humphrey Lyttelton was forced to pre-record the first portion of his BBC radio show, normally broadcast live, amid the emotion of the news.

Over the summer of 1971, the limitations of the Half Dozen's solo power began to show. But then the real coup de grace occurred. Roger Horton booked us back at the 100 Club, but this time to play opposite Terry Lightfoot's wonderfully high-powered band. Terry, a masterful crowd-pleaser, believed in stamping his presence on any evening, and he proceeded to blow us up the 100 Club stairs and away along Oxford Street! His trumpeter was Ian Hunter-Randall, a player of iron lip and merciless range. Micky Cooke's shouting, Abe Lincoln-style trombone was a challenge to most other players in the country. And Paddy Lightfoot's country and western banjo-backed vocals caught the crowd and held it long before we took the stand. In short, we went down like a lead balloon and young, over-intense and emotional as I was then, this felt like the end of the road. A couple of lunchtime gigs for the Jazz Centre Society at the Tennis Club on Haverstock Hill, Hampstead, were also disheartening with a non-existent PA system and a crowd that talked happily through our shaky sets. A few weeks later the Half Dozen disbanded.

Just for a change, I decided it would be fun to blow my cornet without having to conduct musical proceedings as bandleader-arranger and an opportunity presented itself in Dave Claridge's New Orleans Jazz Band, a serious Essex-based group dedicated to the style of George Lewis and Bunk Johnson. Clarinettist Dave recognised that I knew virtually nothing about the precise aesthetics of New Orleans jazz and did a lot to educate me, playing records, talking about the need for musical honesty at all times and presenting me with an autographed copy of a book by Al Rose and Edmond Souchon, *New Orleans Jazz: A Family Album*. He also possessed an anarchic sense of humour. 'Excuse me,' he was liable to hiss across at a soloist making his leisurely way through a slow blues – 'but could you hurry up please?'

His wife Gwen knew a lot about the music too. 'Couldn't you,' she asked me once, listening to my high-speed bebop runs, 'manage to sound a bit *older*?'

At the centre of the rhythm section was banjoist Len Page, who had played for the Crane River Jazz Band back in the 1950s. Len played a straight four to the bar on his banjo, holding down my determined attempts to rush the beat and managing somehow (as Monty Sunshine recalled later) to cross his legs and keep both feet on the floor at the same time!

The Claridge band played regularly around Southend and with it I first experienced the business of hard continuous playing. Three or four choruses of ensemble might be followed by a nod to 'take the first solo'. The result was that gradually I built up stamina, sacrificing, like many jazz players, the care with which classical trumpet players nurture their embouchures. Dave's band played – and drank – hard! Each week we downed pint after pint of draft Guinness with double brandy chasers, willingly raising our glasses to Dave's command, 'Down in one!' It was also at this point that – well under thirty years old – I regularly began to wake up at three o'clock in the morning with heart palpitations until the brandy connection was established and controlled.

Perhaps our finest moment was a day on which Dave organised a full parade band for Rochford Carnival. On that bright, sunny morning, Rochford reverberated to the sound of New Orleans marching music, complete with dancers circling beneath decorated umbrellas. Later that day, in a tiny room above the King's Head, we played one of the most intense musical sessions I remember taking part in anywhere. I wish someone had recorded it. Later, as a professional, I remembered how things were then and often tried to relive the creative ease that flourished in such intimate surroundings.

During this time, Len Page organised my first-ever real recording session for the Nicrosound label owned by Nick Kirby, a music enthusiast who had set up a reel-to-reel tape-recorder and several microphones in his front room. For the session, Len arranged a seven-piece band and we spent the morning blowing our way through a selection of standards. The music sounded good and the resulting tape was sent by Len to *Jazz Journal International* where, to everyone's amazement, it was reviewed by Derrick Stewart-Baxter.

Derrick described me as 'just about the best cornetist to emerge since Ruby Braff'. My first in-print mention by a noted British jazz critic! I read the words one lunchtime and my heart leaped higher than the sun.

One of my principal influences early on had been the red-hot trumpet-cornet of a great British brassman, Freddy Randall and in 1972 I saw him for the first time playing with a classy dixieland band of old colleagues. During the 1940s and 50s, Randall had been Humphrey Lyttelton's most notable rival, playing – unlike Humph who was an Armstrong devotee – in the driving fat-toned Chicago-style of Muggsy Spanier. His long and legendary tenure at Cooks Ferry Inn, Edmonton, had become a regular source for BBC Jazz Club broadcasts.

Apart from being the most daring and spectacular British cornetist of his generation, he was also a gifted black-key pianist who could play almost anything in the key of F-sharp. Freddy wasn't slow to tell stories against himself. On one occasion, he was invited to record a radio session with a large string orchestra but couldn't read a score (or even a single-line trumpet part) and was wary of the challenge.

'I suppose I could do it,' he told the musical director, 'on condition there's a rehearsal first.'

'Certainly Mr Randall. Why don't we arrange to meet at the Maida Vale tennis club opposite the studios around a quarter to two?'

Freddy arrived on time, to be met by his MD. 'Everything's ready and waiting for you to record in the studio.'

'That's all very well,' said Freddy, 'but how about the rehearsal?'

'Oh, Mr Randall,' said his director confidently. 'You don't need to worry about that. I've been rehearsing the strings all morning – and they're note-perfect!'

Freddy played the session to perfection too. The tapes have never been issued but deserve to be. On them, his great generous sound floats in and out of the strings like an old wise master having an intimate conversation with trusted friends.

Freddy's playing in later years was enchantingly different: swiftly slurring runs down the horn dissolving into fulsome vibrato, fuzzy attacks on notes, hoarse half-valving, and fighting phrases which would sometimes self-abort and carry on to some new idea. He could also produce audacious turns of musical wit mid-solo like an old man slyly slipping a witticism past his fellows in the old peoples' home and, from the

late 1960s, after one of several self-imposed retirements, co-
led the Randall-Shepherd All Stars with clarinettist Dave
Shepherd. Sometimes at this point, strangely, his cornet
sounded as if it needed attention. Then, towards the end of
his return to bandleading, Freddy discovered an unchecked
leak in the main slide of his Super Olds cornet. As a result,
tiny fluffs or mispitchings had entered the arena. But somehow they enhanced his performance – it was like listening
to late Billie Holiday, Lester Young or Kenny Ball at more
fallible moments: the occasional errors made Freddy and his
music more identifiable, human and likeable.

He helped me to fall in love with the idea of imperfection
too. Trumpeters like Freddy Randall, Billy Butterfield, or
even the young Warren Vaché, could (like Billie Holiday) turn
vulnerability into an artistic proposition and I began to incor-
porate the idea of 'incorrect', or at least non-orthodox, playing into my own performance. This is risky as listeners must
have travelled the same tracks as you in order to understand
what you're doing. But strangely such musical messages con-
vey themselves from player to listener in a special kind of
extra-verbal communication.

Later Dave Shepherd and Stan Bourke told me a lot more
about Freddy's band in its glory-days: a wild bunch of flaming
youths who travelled in Freddy's bandwagon, known to
British jazz history as the 'Yellow Peril'.

One of the best of many outrageous stories about the young
Randall concerned a regular bandwagon routine: the arseholes game. It sounds mild now, but back around 1950 the
game was quite risqué. Fortified by an evening of good music
supported by whatever was on tap, the band would return to
the bandwagon and get going. The idea was to change one of
the keywords in some respected songtitle to an irreverent
substitute. 'I've Got You Under My Arsehole', Freddy would
lead off. And from then on it was every man for himself. In
glorious ensemble, out came the redesigned numbers. 'Up a
Lazy Arsehole', 'Swing that Arsehole!', 'Stars Fell on

Arseholes!', 'Arseholes by Starlight'. And so on, until inspiration – if that's the word – had been exhausted.

At one point the band was joined by what would now
correctly be called a gifted young 'sideperson'. The fair-of-
face and very junior new arrival briefly prompted some
restraint in the band ribaldry in the Yellow Peril. The good
intentions lasted a night or two, until someone decided that
enough was enough, and it was time to break the new arrival
in the hard way. 'I've Got My Arsehole to Keep Me Warm'
was the joyful cry from some free spirit. And quickly it was
taken up by a string of new suggestions, each more outrageous than the last, until the whole farrago had subsided into
a chorus of breathless giggles. Then when the wagon was
quite silent, a small, silven, and unmistakeably feminine voice
was heard from a back seat.

'You're the Cream in My Arsehole!'

3.

moonlighting

By 1973, word was spreading about my cornet playing and I
was invited to audition for a new traditional band, based in
Essex, to be co-led by banjoist Hugh Rainey and soprano sax-
ophonist Eggy Ley. This was professionalism at a new level.
Hugh had played through all the hit-parading years with Bob
Wallis' Storyville Jazzmen while Eggy had moved on from a
British career in the 1950s to success in Europe, playing and
recording regularly with the veteran saxophonist Benny
Waters. By the time I got to know him, he was based in Essex
and doubling as a producer at British Forces Broadcasting
Service.

My audition was a Sunday lunchtime session: I arrived, cov-
ered in hair and sweat, and blew a loud, unremitting set in
which my lip just held out. Eggy vied heavily for lead in the
ensemble, using his soprano saxophone like a voice to bark
short, peremptory statements which lengthened with passion
to a level of intensity recalling Sidney Bechet.

After my audition, I was convinced I'd failed but a day later
Eggy rang to say I was in. We were to record a session for the
British Forces Broadcasting Service straightaway and everyone was going to look out for work for the band. 'It'll be
called Jazz Legend,' he explained, 'as we'll be playing all the

tunes that are legendary in the jazz repertoire!' It seemed like
a good idea at the time but the publicity value of Eggy and
Hugh's names was lost in the billing: a problem we re-encoun-
tered later with the quartet (co-headed by two famous guitarists Denny Wright and Ike Isaacs) called Velvet in which I
played cornet for four years.

Guests regularly appeared with the band, including Diz
Disley and, at my instigation, Pete Strange who is one of
Britain's great jazz trombonists. I'd heard Pete ten years
before with Bruce Turner's Jump Band and admired him ever
since. The day he appeared with us, however, the entire
rhythm section of Jazz Legend was absent and in desperation
I'd booked 'blood relation' deputies who, it turned out, knew
no dixieland tunes at all. Pete, uncomplaining, played as beautifully as he always does, and over the next thirty years we
would become inseparable friends.

Perhaps our most spectacular guest – at the Reservation
Club, a regular stronghold in Ilford – was George Melly,
before his longterm teaming with John Chilton's
Feetwarmers. George, following public acclaim (plus occasional consternation) for his autobiography *Owning Up*, and a
best-selling album 'Nuts', was a celebrity I longed to meet.
We had an enjoyable first set and afterwards, filled with alcoholic courage, I asked him to sign my prized copy of 'Nuts'
and tried to explain to him that *Owning Up* had done quite a
lot to change my way of living and thinking. In so doing, I
used an obscure term from my library studies.

'It was bibliotherapeutic' I explained.

'Pardon?' said George, completely mystified.

In the early Jazz Legend days I regularly played at The Mitre,
a cavernous tavern on the south side of the Blackwall Tunnel,
notable for its long stage opposite an even longer bar, eighteen feet away. The audience, usually packed tight by the close
of the night, faced the band, soaking up the sound with their
clothing and body heat, and accordingly flattening the room's
acoustics. The result was that any early evening set at the

Mitre rang out with a resonance that would have graced a cathedral; the second, played to a packed crowd, sounded flat and overblown. Nevertheless the music was always spirited and prestigious names played with us.

The Mitre was also notable for two characters. One was the mountainous, ever-courteous cockney docker, Wally Butcher, who sang with whichever band was there ('But beautiful, mate,' was his courtly response whenever invited to sit in). And there was Charlie who owned the pub and soaked up the music as he pulled pints and washed glasses behind the bar.

At the same time, kindly Hugh Rainey invited me to join the regular band at a Basildon pub, the Plough and Tractor, which offered the worst sound I'd yet encountered in a room thanks to thick curtains, carpet and acres of acoustic tiles glued to a low ceiling. The experience felt like playing the cornet with a sock stuffed down its bell in a wardrobe lined with army blankets, but gradually I resigned myself to the room and we managed to hold our crowd.

Hugh told me marvellous stories of his years with the hit-parading Bob Wallis band in the early days of the trad boom in London, as romantic and harum-scarum as the Beatles in Hamburg a year or two later. At one point the bands of both Acker Bilk – just arrived in London from Bristol – and Bob Wallis (as well as agent John Boddy) lived above the shirt factory of industrialist Alan Gatwood in Plaistow, East London. Gatwood had a fondness for the young jazz-crazy men and their girlfriends living in his upstairs premises. 'Bloody jazz moochers,' he would exclaim but never took out eviction orders. Bob Wallis built a still in the room, producing bootleg liquor.

'What's that?' asked the landlord staring into the unholy contents of a tin bath in which a small crop of potatoes floated ominously.

'Irish stew,' Bob explained helpfully.

The entire Wallis band were regular visitors to the Black Lion in Plaistow and after their record of 'Come Along Please' went high in the charts it was re-played every night at closing time, long after every echo of the trad boom had been blown away by the Beatles.

After sessions at the Plough and Tractor came to an end, Hugh transferred operations to play every Wednesday at another local pub, the Essex Arms at Brentwood. In the echoing acoustics of this new venue the band sounded wonderful and I continued to play there until turning professional in 1977.

It seemed that my name was starting to get around the jazz scene as a young dixieland cornetist, full of passion and concerned to improve. The phone began to ring more regularly and one call came from the legendary George Webb inviting me to join his Dixielanders, which I did for a gig or two. Another call came from Colin Symons. A handsome, eligible young raver who died early, Colin was a high-powered drummer who led bands in London from the mid-1960s and I'd seen him in 1971 playing dixieland at the 100 Club. Sometimes he would call me to play at his regular Sunday residency at Olympia and subsequently railroaded me into the idea of joining his band by seductively placing a news item in the jazz pages of *Melody Maker*, 'When Ken Sims leaves the Symons band,' read the piece, 'it is hoped Digby Fairweather will take his place.'

In 1973, Colin, his band and I were invited to Dresden in East Germany to play the celebrated dixieland festival there. The visitors went down well, everyone in the band had a high old time and on the last day we were paid handfuls of money in local currency (valueless west of the Berlin Wall), which had to be spent before we left. I bought an expensive watch (which stopped on the way home and never started again) and what I briefly thought to be a wonderfully fetching Stetson-style hat in deep maroon velvet. Several other members of the band bought one of Dresden's most beautiful products: exquisitely-fashioned children's shoes, hand-made in leather. Once on the bus to the airport, an ill-translated list was handed to Colin. 'The following may not be exported,' he read out, in dismay. 'Oh Christ! Children's leather shoes! I don't believe it.'

Universal groans from his players prompted a quick band-leader's decision. Out came his bass drum from its case and off with its head. In with the shoes, back on with the head and back in the case as our bus rolled in to the airport. Inside the terminal it was the first time any of us remembered the X-ray machine, straddling a conveyor belt lined with officials. Cases were lifted onto the belt to be passed through the machine for internal scrutiny and as Colin neared the front of the queue he and his band were wet with sweaty fear. It was the size of his bass drum that saved us. Too big to pass through the machine, it was allowed through the barrier after a quick look inside the case and an explanation by Colin that, 'there's no way to dismantle this valuable instrument.' It was lucky that none of the officials doubled as drummers.

My beautiful new Stetson made the trip home with me but on the plane I felt that people were taking a second quizzical look. At home, however, on top of the wardrobe, my hat continued to look stylish. 'Well,' I thought one night, 'if George Melly can wear that sort of thing – why shouldn't I?' So I took it to the Mitre one evening and afterwards double-bassist Arthur Bird dropped me as usual at Shenfield Station, deserted in the darkness of one in the morning. As the train headlights appeared in the mid-distance, I slipped my hat on at a jaunty angle, and immediately became aware of footsteps running to join me.

'You are beautiful man!' said a voice to my immediate right and a friendly arm was firmly tucked into mine. 'Let us go home together, now!'

'No – thank you,' I protested, but the new arrival, an Indian man of fifty or so was not to be discouraged, and climbed into the carriage compartment to sit alongside me.

'You are very beautiful man indeed! I have lovely sister at home. Would you like to come and see her? Now, I mean, sir – tonight?'

'No, no, thank you.' I struggled to free my arm from his. 'No! I'm not that kind of man.'

'Ah!' said my new friend, apparently delighted. 'Good! Then come on home with *me*!'

I managed to keep my courtesan at bay until Billericay, next station down and, having wrested myself from his company and changed compartments, I hurled my hat through the train window and into some ploughed field. The birds could build a nest with it.

Colin Symons and I shared gigs over several enjoyable years in the early 1970s: his powerful drumming was reflected in his band, which was high-energy and frequently deafening. Shortly before one of our later meetings at Stannetts, he had acquired the latest in a series of beautiful vintage cars. One weekend morning his jolly public school voice was on the phone. 'I simply *have* to bring it over to show you Dig. Oh, and by the way, I've got the dog with me.'

The dog was a wonderfully mad red setter and hardly had Colin's car halted smoothly at Stannetts before she somer-saulted through the front door then made for the back of the house at high speed. What I didn't know – and nor of course did Colin – was that my father had arranged that day for our septic tank to be emptied, a rare event and certainly not for the faint-hearted. The tempting sight of a swimming hole didn't escape our canine visitor's attention, however, and she managed a couple of triumphant lengths before bounding back to the car, over the elegant leather driver's seat and into the back for a cleansing roll around. Colin – who, by this time, had only just finished saying 'hello' – turned back to his newly acquired vintage beauty in impotent disbelief, followed by horror.

'Well, *fuck* the dog,' he said and without saying goodbye drove off at furious high speed into the middle distance, round the bend and away.

From the early 1970s I'd nurtured an interest in the career of trumpeter Nat Gonella but his records were hard to find.

Then, at last in 1972, I found a purple-label Parlophone hidden near the bottom of a pile of 78s at an antiques centre: 'Don't Cross Your Fingers, Cross Your Heart' backed with 'Stop Beatin' Around the Mulberry Bush'. I was becoming a Gonella convert and fuel was added to the flames when I was given a cassette-full of vintage Gonella 78s by an old friend, Nobby Brand.

A year or so previously I had already made a cheeky phone call to bandleader and record producer Steve Lane to see if he might be interested in a new Nat recording for his Halcyon label. Steve liked the idea but was cautious. 'I don't think you'll get him,' he averred and he was right. On the phone, from Leyland in Lancashire, where he then lived and was playing workingmen's clubs, cockney Nat turned me down flat. But I was determined to know more about this charismatic centrepiece of British Jazz.

Around this time I also played with Eric Silk, the longtime revivalist and banjoist whose band proudly proclaimed itself, 'twenty years traditional'. It was marvellous to be asked to play by men who until recently had been my jazz book heroes! But in this case, the telephone calls came from Eric's father known to all as 'Pop'. Pop Silk had managed his son's band since its foundation. An old army man with a voice that reminded me of Peter Sellers' creation, 'William Mate Cobblers', he would ring me up (I was fairly sure) only when every other trumpet player in London was working. This suspicion was based on something more than paranoia. Halfway through my first job with Eric, I had tentatively asked him if everything was alright.

'It's very good, Digby,' said my new leader cautiously, 'but it's too *florid!*'

Nevertheless, on occasions Pop would ring up with the offer of a job, and he would begin with a greeting that subtly established your status in the Silk musical regime. 'Hello corporal,' he'd begin, or if you were in high favour, 'hello, sergeant!' or even, 'hello, major!' I never made it further than corporal.

Much earlier, in the late 1950s, a very young Pete Strange also worked with Eric. 'One of our regular gigs,' he told me recently, 'was at the Red Lion, Leytonstone. Every week we had a wage slip, which always had deductions. There was a crate of beer by the stage at the Red Lion and every time you took a bottle out, Pop would make a deduction from the fee. But once I got an extra ten bob in my wage packet, and I asked Pop why. 'Well,' he said, 'Eric and I thought you'd turned out extra smart last week.' Which was terrible, because my dad polished my shoes and pressed my trousers and I didn't give him the ten shillings!'

If this were true, then it may have been Pete's only ungenerous gesture in a long career in British jazz. When he played with Silk he was still only seventeen years old and an album of the time reveals in its liner-notes that 'Pete Strange, still under eighteen, has (sshhh!) mainstream tendencies!'

I worked several times with Eric's light-swinging band and in the intervals he regaled me with wonderful stories of the dawn of Britain's jazz revival, of working with the legendary young trumpeter John Haim (whose death was announced in the *Melody Maker* one week before it tragically occurred) and of the fun of being in at the beginning of a great music movement. 'We all used to play on trains,' he told me. 'Once in the compartment, out with the instruments and that was it! One time our clarinettist opened the door and decided to walk round the outside of the carriage, and just as he was gone we went straight into a tunnel. How relieved we were when he reappeared at the other side!'

Trombonist Allan Dean's departure from the Silk band in 1974 played another small role in my jazz journey. Allan had decided to form his own band (which he called the Gene Allen Jazzmen) and was joined by several members of the Silk band including me. The band rehearsed and played dixieland standards in Friday sessions at the Mitre and, one week, Allan asked, 'What are you doing Sundays? Could you play for me regularly?' I was getting a lot of work at this point and my cautious look led Allan to press his advantage, 'It's at the 100

Club. Every Sunday! Roger Horton wants us for a residency! How about that?'

'A residency? Every Sunday? At London's home of traditional jazz? So when do we start?'

'Two weeks' time,' said Allan triumphantly. But after the initial elation passed, I was worried. Would our happy-go-lucky approach survive in such critical surroundings?

Roger Horton, however, had faith in the band and it turned out to be perfect for the Club's free admission night, packed with trippers as well as jazz fans. The combination of stomping traditional jazz and our light approach went down well and the word began to spread: here was a new band worth dropping in to hear. Players and singers came to the 100 Club including Cyril Richardson, closely related to the Richardson gang, who had battled the Kray brothers around London's East End for years. Tall and cockney-courteous, Cyril, who ran a coaching company, regularly bussed nurses from a London hospital to enjoy an evening off with jazz and always serenaded them (and us) with his version of 'Chesapeake Bay'. No-one turned down his ever-modest requests to join the band for a well delivered song! Others who sang with the band from time to time included actors John Turner and Wendy Richards, an excellent dixieland singer who at that point was midway between a supporting role as an actress in the hilarious television comedy 'Are you being served?' and a starring one in a brand-new series, 'East Enders'.

It was always a thrill descending the stairs of the 100 Club to that great echoing tank of a room with its powerful sound system. But gradually the club became familiar territory and for five years the Gene Allen Jazzmen held sway there.

In the mid-1970s I began staying in London regularly with a friend, Chris Watkins. One Sunday lunchtime in the mid-1970s we visited an Indian restaurant near the Tate Gallery, Chris with her neat cropped dark hair and I with generously-flowing gold locks. We sat down and were joined by a waiter with menus. When he saw me, his eyes brightened.

'You are Daltry!' he exclaimed, 'Roger Daltry! From the famous group, the Who! Is it not?'

'No! Really!'

'Oh yes you are, sir!' returned my new friend. 'But you wish privacy! This I understand!'

Our waiter took our orders, then left us in peace. But when I paid our bill before departing, a bright parcel two inches wide, wrapped in soft silver foil, was pressed into my hand.

'This is a present for you! For you, Mr. Daltry!'

Gingerly I opened the parcel. It was an enormous wedge of marijuana.

'No, no, honestly,' I said.

'For you, Mr Daltry,' insisted the waiter. 'Me and my family, we are great fans of you and your wonderful group! One day we would all like to come and see you too!'

'On a concert?' I said, deciding it was time to get into the spirit of the thing.

'No, no Mr Daltry. At home! I bring family to see you at home! Now you must give me your address!' A piece of paper and pen appeared on the table at my side.

For some unaccountable reason, I found myself writing down the first address I could think of: 15 River View Mansions, Hammersmith. This, I remembered as we were leaving, was the London home of my good friend, the American cornetist Dick Sudhalter – just a mile or two up the Thames from the Tate Gallery.

'Thank you, Mr Daltry,' I heard the voice as we left. 'Thank you. We come and see you soon.'

Many years later I nervously enquired whether or not Dick had received unexpected visitors, but luckily no-one had arrived.

One day, soon after this, Charlie at the Mitre rang up in a panic. 'Listen, Digby,' he said. 'Monty Sunshine can't play tonight and I haven't got a band. If I give you his money, can you put one together in a hurry?'

Monty Sunshine went out for good money. So here was a dream opportunity: I could assemble some of the men whose music I'd admired so much over the years. I rang Tony Milliner, longtime colleague of Scottish clarinettist Sandy Brown, and he said yes. So, to my delight, did Henry Mackenzie, Ted Heath's master clarinettist of twenty or more years. Brian Lemon – unquestionably Britain's most eminent mainstream pianist – was free. So was Phil Franklyn, one of the more polished dixieland-to-swing drummers of the day. And to complete the band I called bassist Ron Russell, whose name I knew well for fine dixieland music in south London.

The rhythm section, graced by Brian Lemon's superlative piano playing, was a dream come true and from that day Brian would be a friend for life. Henry and Tony were superior to almost any players I'd shared a stand with up until then and blithely I blew my way through an evening made in musical heaven. The Mitre's crowd, unused to polished swing-to-mainstream jazz (and most of them expecting Monty Sunshine anyhow) were less than bowled over, and so, unfortunately, was Charlie who reluctantly handed over our fee. But, unrepentantly, I thought, 'This is good!'

By now, I had found a sturdy friend in Alex Welsh. His regular phone calls to the music library at Southend between 1973 and 1976 were filled with warmth and wisdom. In between asking me how I was getting on with my youthful career, he talked regularly and with fondness of Al Jolson, Gene Kelly and Judy Garland, 'There's a lot of Broadway in me!' Alex admitted.

Increasingly often, too, his calls were to ask if I could deputise with his band. Alex was gradually becoming unwell and had returned from a visit to East Germany with a virus producing a wet rash, making it impossible for him to wear clothing, let alone work up a sweat blowing his cornet on the stand. There had also been disturbing reports that – like Kenny Ball a few years earlier – he had briefly suffered crippling lip-trouble, causing concern and dismay amongst his sidemen. Nevertheless, one of Alex's most spectacular phone calls came in 1974. 'What are you doing tomorrow

night, lad? Come and play with me at the Queen Elizabeth
Hall!'

London's second biggest concert hall after the Royal
Festival was a premier venue and this concert – one of many
promoted by Michael Webber and Arthur Thompson – was
to honour Alex's twentieth anniversary as a bandleader. This
was evidence that I had joined the select (and much envied)
group of 'friends of Alex Welsh', a salon of outstanding players. The following morning I warmed up gently, polished my
cornet and shoes and spent the rest of the time working up a
fever of excitement.

I was to share the bill as guest with the great tenorist Danny
Moss, guitarist Diz Disley and tap dancer Will Gaines whom
Alex had discovered when he danced across a service station
forecourt to fill the Welsh bandwagon with petrol in
Lancashire. The concert attracted a packed house, Danny
played a ravishing ballad, Diz shared a duet with Alex
on 'Gone Fishin'' with special patter thrown in, and then
it was my turn. I led the band through Louis Armstrong's
'Once in a While', managing a reasonably creditable stop-
chorus and the waves of applause were intoxicating. The
night, for me, can never be forgotten but lunchtime next day
there came a small salutary reminder of the fleeting nature of
success. Once again I crossed Waterloo Bridge, past the
Queen Elizabeth Hall, this time to play un-noticed, with
drummer Ian Bell's band, to less than a dozen people in the
Stamford Arms.

After our night at the Queen Elizabeth Hall, Alex invited me
to join him regularly on South Bank stages for Michael
Webber and one day, before such a show, I went to his flat to
find him in his regularly adopted bandleader's position, sitting on the floor, on the phone, surrounded by contracts and
a map of England, and drinking vodka. Occasionally, as his
deputy, I travelled in the Welsh bandwagon too and became
familiar with the small but inflexible rules of on-the-road life.
Every member had his own seat; sit in someone's place by

mistake and you were gently but firmly re-directed. Then there was the humour which flared like marsh-gas whenever the Welsh men were together. John Barnes, who loves joke-shops, had bought a hideous plastic mask in Glasgow and christened him Angus Goodaye.

'Why do you call him Goodaye?' I asked.

'Well,' said John, 'whenever the Alex Welsh band played Glasgow we'd be drinking afterwards with punters and ask, "what did you think of the show?" And the answer was always the same: "Good! Aye!"'

Goodaye occasionally joined the band for a drink in the pub en route to work. If he were otherwise engaged, however, the Welsh men would create a deputy, using Lennie Hastings' wig, bassist Ron Mathewson's false eye and John Barnes' false teeth. The new member would be hospitably included in every round until it was time to climb back into the bandwagon.

The band played at the Glasgow Empire where, it was said, 'if they liked you they let you live'. Alex disliked playing Glasgow and Edinburgh. Back there, he was still the ambitious local lad who had to prove himself with every performance after success down in the softbacked South. 'You're never a hero in your hometown, lad.' Alex warned me. 'Remember that!'

One of my first trips in the Welsh bandwagon was to Newcastle City Hall to play in a concert starring Ruby Braff, the greatest jazz cornetist in the world, and to everyone's delight Ruby had decided to travel with us for the long drive from London. During the journey my cornet-idol talked about his long career and discussed the exquisite recordings by the quartet he had led for a time with guitarist George Barnes. Ruby had failed to stay friends with Barnes but reluctantly conceded of their recordings, 'Yeah, they're pretty!'

Once at the hall, Ruby announced no tunes but simply played them: a ravishing version of 'The Man That Got Away' remained unaccompanied as no-one else knew it. My role, as I watched him finger his valves, was principally to whisper the keys of Ruby's selections to my friends on the stand. It was a wonderful concert and, making our way back to the hotel, I found myself in the unique position of walking up a Newcastle street, arm-in-arm with Ruby, singing the 'Lambeth Walk'.

Next day he made his way back to London by train and I travelled on with the Welsh Band to play another concert at the Theatre in the Forest, Cumbria. During the overnight ride home I was, for the first time, witness to one of the high-octane arguments that could erupt in the Welsh bandwagon at a moment's notice. On one occasion tenorist Al Gay, having been invited to join Alex's band, turned down the offer with a now celebrated reply.

'I'd like to,' said Al, 'but I can't fight!'

Alex ran his band as a musical and financial co-operative: every member was paid equally and had an equal say in band policy. Consequently – and because there were strong characters in Alex's ranks – rows could be frighteningly intense. There had been one major argument ten minutes before the band's Dresden Concert of 1971, which some aficionados call Alex Welsh's greatest recording ever.

'There we were,' Roy Williams told me later, 'squaring up to one another over something or another. "Right you bastard, you're fired." And so on. Real abuse! And then, ten minutes later there we were on the stand, arms around each others' shoulders, singing 'Dapper Dan'! And afterwards – all forgotten of course!' He laughed at the memory.

Unlike many bandleaders, Alex Welsh never employed a fulltime agent. On behalf of his 'boys' he filled his datesheet single-handed, a task which distracted him mentally from the end-product of the day – a relaxed performance – and no doubt re-directed him to his vodka bottle, 'All I ever wanted to do was play 'Jazz Band Ball',' he would say ruefully. 'But sometimes, by the time I get on the stand, the last thing I feel like is a cornet player.' As the years drew on, I came to sympathise with Alex's predicament, recognising it as a real and common problem. And eventually, temperament, internal strife and Alex's progressively heavy drinking would bring this great band down.

Meantime, in 1975, John Barnes rang up, 'Would you like to make a record with the Welsh band?'

'Of course I would!' I stuttered.

'Fine,' said John calmly. 'Alex can't do it as he's under contract to Black Lion so he's suggested you. We'll be recording at Chappells and there might be a rehearsal, if you can make it, at New Merlins Cave, Clerkenwell, to run through a couple of things.'

'Anything you say,' I managed to respond.

'Fine. And by the way, the fee is twenty-six pounds for the day.'

'When,' I said in all seriousness, 'do I pay you?'

The recording session went well enough and the album was reissued in 1998 by Lake Records in their 'British Jazz Heritage' series – it was strange to see my recent past turning into some sort of local jazz history. The album continues to get good reviews and few people have noticed that on the track 'You Took Advantage of Me' the cornetist plays the middle eight to 'Wrap Your Troubles in Dreams' by mistake. Take a listen!

Alex was regularly in touch from then on and once rang up to ask if I would substitute for him at a 'Band Parade' recording for Radio 2. This was my first broadcast. It was a hot day but Alex showed up to keep me company, as well as an ear and eye on things. After two or three tracks had gone down in one take (the Welsh band's normally note-perfect standard of recording) I innocently asked if I might take a swig from the water Alex was carrying in a blue Volvic bottle. After a pause he agreed and I found myself taking a generous gulp of vodka only lightly diluted with lemonade. What I hadn't realised then was how heavily Alex drank the clean spirit that doesn't give you a hangover. Over the years though it was to pay him a terrible revenge.

***

Lennie Hastings

Double-bassist Ron Russell was a focus for classy main-stream jazz activity in south London in the mid-1970s and in 1975, after the sublimely-gifted trumpeter Colin Smith decided to stop playing for his regular sessions, he offered me a one-night tryout before inviting me to join his band full-time. This was my most exciting career step since joining Jazz Legend four years before. Now I was to play two regular jobs a week in the very best of British swing company at a south London pub, the Chinbrooke, and a regular Monday residency in the Glaziers' Club at Crystal Palace Football Club.

The band at the time contained Al Gay or Dave Jones (clarinet); Pete Strange (trombone); Stan Greig, Brian Lemon or Keith Ingham (piano); Ron (bass) and, regularly, Lennie Hastings (drums) – without question, the greatest dixieland drummer in the country.

I was delighted when Ron announced one evening, with his normal nonchalance, 'Lennie's on drums tonight.' Seconds later the door of the club crashed open as a scarlet bass drum rolled at high speed across the floor, followed at double speed by the outline of a man who hurled himself into the lavatory. This was Lennie, who emerged five minutes later, breathless but relieved.

'Made it!' he said triumphantly.

Lennie had lived long and hard, and his standard order at the bar – by now comprising, 'a pint of rough cider, and a large brandy, cock! Oh and a Pernod (but I'll pay for the Pernod),' – was pushing his digestive system to organised rebellion. Lennie paid his fellow players the compliment of absolute honesty and one night at the Glaziers Club I rightly came in for a ticking off. My trumpet-lead on an old dixieland standard, 'Fidgety Feet', had descended into ornate strings of inappropriate notes leaving nowhere free for my fellow improvisers to play their parts. Lennie cornered me at the bar at half-time.

'I don't want to upset you, mate,' he said, 'but listen. All that ornate crap you're playing. It's all fucking wrong. Why can't you just play the lead?'

I can't remember how I responded, beyond apologies. But, in terms of dixieland proper, Lennie was absolutely right. The criticism I'd received was devastating from such a role-model but hereafter my playing became a little more guarded and qualified in exuberance as well as a lot more credible to long-time listeners to dixieland. In short, the question of 'taste' was consciously entering my music for the first time.

Another friend I acquired in the Ron Russell band was Keith Ingham, a pianist of international standard. At this time he had formed a personal and musical duo with the singer Susannah McCorkle and they were living in Earls Court. Keith's piano technique was as awesome as his intellect; a multi-linguist, he had a degree from Oxford in Mandarin Chinese and could rattle through the *Times* cross-word in five minutes. On the piano, he could as easily reel off traditional selections – 'Honky Tonk Train Blues' or 'Echo of Spring' – as he could produce a convincing impression of McCoy Tyner or Thelonious Monk. When not playing piano, he worked for Air France as a bookings representative and brought to this job an admirable set of values. Having heard that a leading rock star, while drunk en route to a concert, had hit a stewardess, Keith booked the star's entire group into the middle of nowhere, then cancelled their connection. Faced with complaints as a result of such initiatives he would politely request his callers to hold on for a moment, and then transfer them to the English cricket scores!

We met regularly at Crystal Palace, often consuming a huge (and potentially damaging) curry before walking on to the nearby clubhouse. Keith, as well as being a marvellous player, was totally in love with jazz and brought to the music a sense of continuous inquiry that separated him from all but a handful of jazz pianists in Britain. Faced with an unfamiliar tune (a rare occurrence) he would search out recordings or sheet music and arrive the following week with everything learned, including the verse, in all keys. In 1977, Keith emigrated to America, played with Benny Goodman and moved to the top echelons of America's jazz society.

Ron Russell's band never became a famous group in national jazz terms but it was a university of excellence. All its players cared deeply for the ethos of real dixieland music and together we sought out unfamiliar repertoire. We also made an album dedicated to our Monday residency called 'Jazz at the Palace'. One Wednesday, at our other regular venue, the Chinbrooke in Grove Park, there was no sign of a clarinettist. 'Who's playing for us this week?' I enquired and Ron said, quite casually, 'Oh – Dave Shepherd's coming over.'

Shepherd was Freddy Randall's lifelong colleague and had led his own legendary quintet from 1954, broadcasting on a weekly basis for Radio 2 and touring with Teddy Wilson. He arrived soon after and we took the stand. Dave was used to the 'busy', multi-noted, lead cornet of Freddy Randall, a style I still loved and fell back into from time to time, and he could miraculously find a complementary part in the ensemble, proceeding from there into solos which possessed all the elegance and regular heat of Benny Goodman. Over the years Dave was very kind to me, we became close colleagues and friends and would collaborate on other projects including, from 1994, the Great British Jazz Band. Dave is the finest swing clarinettist in the country, and, perhaps since Artie Shaw took to writing books and Benny Goodman went aloft, the best in the world.

In 1976 Ron Russell's band made the first of its Mediterranean cruises for Chandris on the liner *Ellinis*. This time John Barnes came with us to play clarinet.

'Don't be surprised,' he told us on deck one day, 'because I won't be! I think I'm going to be fired from Alex Welsh's band when I get home.'

'Oh no,' we said. But he was. Later on, Alex told me, 'I had a week of sleepless nights before I could make up my mind to sack John.'

But, despite this shadow over John's head, it was a marvellous cruise with Pete Strange, John Richardson, Keith Ingham and Susannah McCorkle joining the band. Our final stop was Cadiz and I wandered along the foreshore with its waving palm trees, wondering whether Gil Evans had seen this memorable view and its maids before he wrote his masterpiece for Miles Davis.

An unofficial guest on board was the French trumpeter Jean-Loup Longnon, son of Lionel Hampton's famous cornetman Guy Longnon. Built like Dizzy Gillespie with horn to match, Jean-Loup bounded into our company early on, dressed in a spectacular kaftan, and regularly thereafter with the belling cry of, 'Let us go make jam!' at most hours of the day and night.

At this point the very sprauncy Portman Hotel in Portman Square held weekly jazz brunches and I played a lot of them with Ron Russell and various groups of my own. Famous visitors often came in but our most remarkable guest arrived one day when lunch was almost over. I opened my eyes at the end of a solo with Ron's band and there – no more than two feet from my cornet-bell – was Dizzy Gillespie!

John Barnes seized a pause in the music to explain. 'Dizzy's here because I know where his guru's buried. You know Dizzy is a B'hai? Well his guru, Shogun Effendi died in England. They had to bury him within six hours and so he's in a cemetery near Southgate, where I used to work. We're going across to see him. Would you like to come?'

So Dizzy, John and I drove across London together. Dizzy was friendly, approachable and happy to answer questions. I asked him about Charlie Parker and touched gingerly, in passing, on Ross Russell's biography, *Bird Lives!*, which maximised Parker's central contribution to bebop, while making less than it might of Dizzy's own. Dizzy agreed that the portrait was sanctified to extreme levels.

'That's right. Charlie Parker was a man. Just a man!'

When we arrived at the cemetery, John and I sat in the car while Dizzy walked out in the evening sun to stand for several minutes meditating at Shogun's graveside. On the way home he talked happily again, occasionally falling asleep for twenty seconds or so before picking up the conversation where it had left off.

By now, as he'd predicted, John Barnes was out of Alex Welsh's band. Roy Williams followed soon after, missing the close-knit musical frame that the two of them had built around their leader. At last, it was claimed, Alex had what he always wanted, a true dixieland band with Al Gay playing clarinet and tenor and initially Campbell Burnap, and later Micky Cooke, playing trombone. I carried on deputising for Alex from time to time and on one occasion, while playing on the 'Jersey Jazz Boat', arrived in the ship's lounge to find the Welsh men duly seated around a table. From their midst came a small voice: 'Hello, lad!'

It was Alex's unmistakeable greeting but, to begin with, I had missed the shrunken figure between two sidemen at the table. My friend seemed to have halved in size, reduced almost to a rubicund circular-faced dwarf. Vodka was taking its toll.

The Jersey Jazz Boats – which later turned into the Jersey Jazz Festivals – were little short of pleasurable orgies. Most visitors were out for a good time, and the musicians were the centre of attention. One member of the Welsh band (in a famous escapade) spotted an attractive stranger, raced to the bedroom and made it back to the stand, all in the course of a six-minute piano feature by Fred Hunt. Fred himself would simply play on after the band's concert, fortified by Gauloises and triple whiskies until the last exhausted listeners had made for bed. Then he would drink 'one for the stairs' and stagger to oblivion.

Meantime, Ron Russell's band recorded for BBC's 'Sounds of Jazz' and regularly broadcast for Capital Radio. We also played a shortlived residency at the Telegraph in Brixton, a music pub which budgeted for guests. One was Bud Freeman, who played inimitably and personified charm. Another was Humphrey Lyttelton who arrived from another job and calmly consumed an enormous T-bone steak before placing knife and fork together, picking up his horn and mounting the stand without pause to play a powerhouse set.

One session during this residency was particularly memorable. Acker Bilk was our Sunday lunchtime guest and had travelled from Barnet with Ron. The two of them had persuaded an off-licence, closed for Sunday, to open up specially in honour of the star and bought a multi-pack of Carlsberg Special lager to drink before the music got started. Later on, after it was over, Acker, ever genial and approachable, invited us all to the bar to drink. By six o'clock the band's cornetist was distinctly unsteady and vaguely aware that work was not yet over for the day.

'Acker,' I managed to say with some difficulty, 'I have to be going! I'm due at the 100 Club with the Gene Allen Jazzmen at eight.'

'No problem, cock,' said Acker, 'I'll have my driver drop you off.' Once in Oxford Street, underneath a swaying sky, I was aware of the need for emergency measures, and made for a curry house in Berwick Street. Coffee might have helped. But a full-scale Indian meal induced both a terminal desire for sleep and what felt like a concrete block just under my diaphragm. Somehow I staggered across Oxford Street and made my way down the steps to the basement at number 100 to see a front row of seats fully occupied by semi-familiar figures.

'Hello,' said a voice joined by others. 'How are you?' And something very close to a cheer went up.

It was several members of the Fairweather family plus friends, out for the evening to hear their new-star relation. Heroically they sat while I flubbed through a set with tired lip, invading hangover – and a stomachful of curry – before making their excuses and departing in search of real West End entertainment.

In 1976 Ron Russell's band made another trip abroad at the invitation of Ron's friend and business colleague, Ted Easton. This time we went to Scheveningen on the Hook of Holland. In 1932 Ray Noble's band had visited there to play at the Kurhaus and Nat Gonella had been one of the stars in the band. When Nat came back to the Kurhaus in 1975 as part of his later burst of glory, Easton had the good idea of crowning him 'King of Jazz'. The following year, the worthy winner was Beryl Bryden – Britain's 'Queen of the Blues'.

Beryl was a marvellous entertainer and a gifted artist. She was also a devoted deep-sea diver and one of her many spectacular souvenirs was a film of herself playing the washboard one hundred feet under water. On this occasion accompanying Beryl, however, we found ourselves on a seafront bandstand. As usual she had carefully selected her programme, passing out chords cards and arrangements.

'And,' she suggested, 'when I sing 'West End Blues', I'd like to ask for one minute's silence in respect for Louis Armstrong before we begin. Is that alright with you all?'

Certainly! The only problem was that the bandstand's antique public address system may have been the only one in existence that, as in Ronnie Scott's one-liner, 'actually made you sound softer!' Undeterred, Beryl made her appeal for silence into the microphone but the excellence of sentiment and subject were lost to the world as totally as if she'd tapped it out in Morse code on the bandstand rail. Passers-by continued their conversations, what audience there was failed to get the message and even the Ron Russell band – full of high spirits and beer – missed its cue, talking, laughing and generally behaving like a pack of ex-schoolboys out on a holiday trip.

Beryl was rightly dismayed and when the concert was over made her professional exhortation to put matters right.

Beryl Bryden

'Boys! *Please* – pay attention when I ask for that minute's silence. Thank you!' Next day, the band was on its guard, waiting for the barely audible rattle of sound that constituted Beryl's request for silence.

When it came we all stood to attention, heads bowed, and the audience, aware of the situation or not, obediently followed suit. All was reverentially still until, quite without warning, Tony Allen fell off his drum stool in a paroxysm of noisy laughter. Ignoring warning looks, he pointed with a drumstick to John Barnes who, from beyond the bandstand railings, was indicating manically skyward and valiantly subduing laughter. Members of the Ron Russell band followed his pointing arm across the Scheveningen bay to a bi-plane dragging an impressively long banner which read *'Durex, the best for you!'*

After this, poor Beryl abandoned her idea. I was in touch with her for the next twenty years. Indomitably cheerful and optimistic for all of her life, she fought cancer for six years from 1992, discharging herself from a London hospital that year, after six debilitating weeks of treatment, to sing at a

Beryl's picture of me

concert with the Alex Welsh Reunion Band for Tim Lord at the Ludlow Jazz Festival. The next morning we travelled back to London together and I found out more about her: a big-hearted lady who travelled hundreds of miles to scuba-dive and loved life and all its colours.

For years I saw her regularly at the BBC Jazz Society and on gigs elsewhere. She toured Europe with fine bands and I grew to love her well-crafted act: each song delineated in chord-symbols for the band members on small rectangular cards known with affection (and occasional resignation) as 'Beryl's beer mats'. There would be an up-tempo tune to open, then a blues showcasing her great, frank, contralto voice with its unmistakeable anglicised overtones. Then, to top the set, her superb silver-plated washboard would be unwrapped from its carefully crafted cloth cover. The accompanying production of thimbles – previously secreted in her capacious brassiere – always caused merriment.

'Need any help?' Roy Williams would call across.

One day Beryl asked me, 'Have you got a decent photograph of yourself?'

'I think I can find one. Why do you ask?'

'I thought I'd do a sketch of you!'

This was quite a compliment. Her previous wonderful

drawings of Louis Armstrong, Bessie Smith, Lionel Hampton and others had found their way into her 'Giants of Jazz' calendar and onto the walls in an impressive one woman gallery for the National Jazz Archive. We found a suitable snapshot and Beryl went to work, checking draft efforts with me. Finally she arrived at a meeting of the BBC Jazz Society with a large artist's folder. 'There you are,' she said. It was a beautiful pencil portrait. Beryl died on 14th July 1998. Her agent Jack Higgins had the last word. 'I can see the morning in heaven – there's Beryl bicycling furiously across heaven. And, over on a cloud, Louis and all his friends saying, "Dig, you cats! Here comes Beryl!"'

In the 1970s, around the first time that I met Beryl, the Digby Fairweather publicity machine took off at full speed. Most jazz musicians know that to stay popular you must try to keep your name before the public and there existed free advertising possibilities in the pages of *Melody Maker*. Week by week they generously reported jazz news, published interviews and features, and assembled a 'What's On' column. So, once a week Chris Allen, my colleague in the music library, listed all my dates – often six a week – and sent them off to jazz editor Max Jones who entered them in his column and diary. My name therefore appeared with relentless regularity in these listings and from time to time I would shamelessly include sessions in which I had no more than a minor supportive role. Stan Greig's wonderful London Jazz Big Band, for example, found itself billed 'with Digby Fairweather' – never more than a fortunate deputy on any occasion.

I was playing well, nevertheless, and realised that – to get known – efficient marketing of my name was part of the deal. Nowadays that philosophy is well-acknowledged in jazz circles: organisations such as Jazz Services publish booklets on the subject. But such methods were less well-established back then and it may have been that, unwittingly, I set a precedent. Marketing yourself as a jazz musician is harder now I think.

Melody Maker – once the jazzman's weekly bible – and its faithful loving scribe Max Jones are sadly missed and have never been fully replaced.

Throughout this period I was still working in the library. On many days I sat in the café next door to our Music and Arts Department while devouring great new jazz biographies: Richard Sudhalter's meticulously detailed *Bix, Man and Legend*, Ross Russell's technicolour *Bird Lives!* and Eddie Condon's beautiful and touching *Scrapbook of Jazz*. This was the era of fine jazz bibliography and – to some degree – the twilight of the classic jazz years. It was also in the library, around 1975, that I had what must be my shortest ever telephone conversation: 'Monty Sunshine here. Can you go to Germany tomorrow?'

'Er... No! Sorry!'

'OK!' Click. And that was that.

4.

how to give up a day job

By mid-1976 it was clear that I was ready, in principle, to make the move to professional jazz. My diary was full of work involving people whose company only six years before had been a dream. That year I made my first-ever live broadcast for the BBC's 'Sounds of Jazz' with Lennie Hastings' band. Then Keith Nichols, who nurtured my early career, invited me to Hamburg to make an album as guest trumpet soloist with the Pasadena Roof Orchestra. But I was still unsure whether to give up my daytime job. My whole life seemed to have been spent getting ready to make this move. And by now thirty years had gone by.

One late autumn evening sometime before seven o'clock, in the Music and Arts Department I'd helped to bring into being in Southend Library, the lights had gone on. Soft reflections shone in the shaded windows as eventide fell. Gentle music drifted from the headset by the turntable. I liked my librarian lifestyle and heard my quiet inner-self say, 'This feels like home.'

This was the straight life advocated by my mother and father, grandparents and school. At school, around 1962, a 'careers convention' had been held. Amid hastily erected cubicles advertising the joys of banking, the Civil Service (and maybe librarianship too), boys were encouraged to peer uncertainly into their future. I'd entered one such area for advice to ask, 'What are the chances of making a living in jazz?' And the answer was simple: 'None.'

I'd grown up torn between the dual demands of duty and motivation, convinced that whatever I spent my time doing for love, something else must be done as well, for the sake of the real world. But I was being drawn irresistibly to the art I loved and towards making a total commitment to a single lifestyle as a professional musician, based not upon any sort of sound training, such as that received by young musicians in the National Youth Jazz Orchestra, but simply on a private desire, an inward rebellion against childhood indoctrination: a feeling, simply, that jazz was where I wished, perhaps had, to be. Lauren Bacall once said of the beginning of her film career, 'I was very lucky. I think it's very fortunate to know what you want to do with your life!'

There was really no-one to help sort out my thoughts. Ena, ever my supporter, would always say, 'You must do what you want to do, that's all that matters.' My father was less pliable. 'If you do this,' he had said to me one evening not long before, 'you do it without my help, my blessing, or my support!' For a sensitive young man, this felt akin to the Jewish act of *shiva*: casting a member out and away from the family bosom for wrongdoing. And there remained the aggravating thought that jazz wasn't serious, just a part-time pleasure to be squashed into spare hours after the serious business of earning daily bread. No doubt more considerable artists – Louis Armstrong, Dizzy Gillespie or Clifford Brown for example – enjoyed different views.

I only knew that the music was calling me away from that endless queue of library 'readers' with their books and records; the queue that stretched until I was sixty-five years old and then disappeared without trace, along with my life. So, in the top office I sought out my good friend, deputy librarian Frank Easton, and told him all about my dreams.

'Well,' said Frank, after a pause, 'If you were forty I'd say 'definitely no'. But as you're only thirty – is that right? – I think there's probably still time. Perhaps you should go after your dream. Perhaps you should.'

I thought over Frank's advice and decided he must be right. Of course I could handle things. So I wrote a letter of resignation and left it on his desk. Back down at the music desk I pondered over my decision and turned to confide in my colleague Chris Allen, 'You know, Chris, if there's one thing that ever would get me out of the jazz business it would be the loneliness.'

Back then, that was possibly my truest realisation so far. Eleven years had been spent enjoying the pleasantly level society of librarians. If I came into work after playing badly the night before, that was regrettable so far as I was concerned, but it mattered nothing as I still had a day job! And if I agonised to some colleague over missing that last top C, I'd be directed in short order to something far more essential to my daytime world, like sending out overdue cards for books kept over time. The very best kind of corrective therapy!

At close quarters the jazz world had already taken on cartoon aspects, peopled by a society that up to now fitted itself comfortably into spare hours. I wanted to play more, to explore the seductive landscape of fulltime jazz. But amid that landscape were threatening visions, everything from blunt critics to suspect agents. As a fulltime jazzman – even one whose creative head was still in the clouds – I knew that I'd be no more than jobbing labour, devoid of status, sick pay and paid holidays.

I wasn't even sure that my kindly, supportive compadres-to-be were complete blood brothers, and for the next few years my suspicions tended to firm up. British jazz musicians talked enthusiastically about themselves as 'the chaps!' – a phrase that I hadn't heard – or felt inclined to use – since reading Billy Bunter tales as a boy. Others I knew addressed each other – apparently seriously – as 'dear boy'. Many watched cricket, football or tennis: nothing wrong with that, except that I found sport a bore. And very few jazz musicians either identified with, or even liked, the pop music of the 1960s that I'd grown up with. Plainly, to join this society at all I'd have to draw in my horns and think differently. But perhaps, I told myself, this was all no more than a matter of minor adjustments. This was self-deception, however.

Nevertheless, as the year progressed, I found an accountant, paid off all my HP commitments and accumulated five hundred pounds: quite a comfortable amount at that time with which to start a new life! Just before I left Southend Library, one of my Wednesday sessions with Ron Russell's band at the Chinbrooke included Ronnie Gleaves, a skilled vibraphonist who played piano too, and somewhere between our two sets I told him about my plans to make it as a professional. Dressed as usual in bow tie and an evening jacket, he faced me squarely, placing his hands on my shoulders.

'Well, I'll tell you, Digby,' he pronounced, delivering a life-long philosophy. 'You've got to have a lot of luck in this game. Or you might as well say fuck it!'

So at last the day approached when I would say good bye to nine-to-five. A jazzman at last! All my dreams were about to fulfil their most threatening promise – by coming true. As the library doors swung shut behind me, I was aware of an enveloping blanket of security pulled abruptly away and an iron band of damaging pressure clamped in its place.

From here, time would defocus, weekends would disappear, the timetable of working hours would fade away and holidays were no longer applicable, as life was now – presumably – one long working holiday. Most of the disciplines of my first thirty years were about to evaporate and I would have to get used to a self-appointed schedule. No longer was my life to be controlled by others: no assistants to consider, no chief to satisfy, no salary. The beaming youth who spent to the hilt and was always first to the bar to buy his round would have to undergo a character change. There would be periods from this time and after that I couldn't recall at all. 'You must remember,' friends would say later, in happier years. 'We saw you at such and such a theatre, or jazz club or holiday camp.'

'Did you?' I would query. 'You know, I honestly can't remember anything about that at all.' Selective memory took over and details were lost amid a frenetic journey from one hasty project to the next.

The night I left the library, my girlfriend Chris Watkins was ill in our flat at Forest Gate, 'Can you manage on your own?' she croaked as I fussed around, dropping my farewell gifts and changing my clothes in order to head for the Prospect of Whitby. For weeks now I had played at this ancient venue in Wapping with Alvin Roy's band on Saturdays, tearing up the room with carefree daredevil trumpet playing which made most of my British colleagues sound slow in comparison. 'Tonight, though,' a small alien voice within me warned, 'things are different. Aren't they? Tonight you've got to be better. Tonight – and from now on too. Just remember!'

And of course, from then on, I could not forget. That very night a strain crept into my performance that would take years to disappear.

For two or three years thereafter I did myself few favours on the jazz scene. The pressures of the jazz life caused me to start playing too hard for comfort and prompted spells of agoraphobia and tachycardia, two complaints I wouldn't have heard of two years earlier. I became rather hard to live with too, but also made new friends, and one of them was record producer Alan Bates. To tide myself over the leap to freelance professional musician status, I had approached Alan at Black Lion Records. Would he, I wondered, consider the possibility of using me as a freelance assistant with the company?

'Certainly,' said Alan. 'You can work the hours you want and record whoever you want, plus make records yourself!'

This was an offer from heaven, but nonetheless I wrote my new employer a lengthy letter stipulating so many hours a week, at this much, over such and such a period: a set of conditions which Alan typically – and sensibly – ignored completely. He also cancelled our first 'official' week of work, a decision that left my nerves twanging like banjo strings. But at last, on a newly arranged day, I arrived at Alan's home near Black Lion Mews in Hammersmith and worked there for the next few months, setting up recording sessions and writing endless sleevenotes.

One afternoon, Alan tried to teach me the tricky art of tape editing and perhaps unwisely suggested that I practise by editing applause. He watched in growing frustration as stretches of cut tape started to decorate the tape-decks and floor. Matters were made worse as the album concerned was a live recording of Alex Welsh's 1971 Dresden concert that would, after Alan's hasty salvage, become a classic.

At lunchtime, we went regularly to the Black Lion pub and became friends, despite a number of errors of mine. One particular problem was his girlfriends. Alan is now happily married but at that time my new employer was single and had two French mistresses indistinguishable (for me at least) on the phone. 'Nice to see you earlier on,' I said one midday morning, unfortunately to the wrong one! *Comme d'habitude*, Alan bore the problem with resignation!

He also gave me the chance to produce albums, usually recorded at the Radio Luxembourg studios in Mayfair. Most ambitiously of all, we co-organised a complete British Jazz Week at the 100 Club, all of which Alan recorded and which has yet to be issued on CD. This involved some imaginative presentations and once again, in my insatiable desire to meet the legendary Nat Gonella, I rang to ask if he'd be prepared to make an appearance on this night and offered big money. 'I'm sorry, mate,' said Nat, 'but I haven't played recently. And I don't really want to be bothered to come down to London.' Here was a man who wanted no part of a career encore, at least for now.

Another client for Black Lion was New Orleans figurehead Ken Colyer, known as 'The Guv'nor'. I rang him and asked if he'd like to record at Radio Luxembourg.

'Not fuckin' much! Can't stand the fuckin' acoustics. Do it at the fuckin' 100 Club – that'd be fuckin' better!' So that was agreed.

I always loved Ken Colyer – the purity of his musical motives, leading a great New Orleans band, his glass-clear tone, but his last years were sad. He produced a poignant autobiography, *When Dreams Are in the Dust,* plainly expressing disillusion at the battle of the New Orleans Revival won and lost.

Stomach cancer returned and his last months were spent in France. Friends sent letters telling him how much he was missed in Britain but some were returned,

Ken Colyer

rubber-stamped with the word 'Bollocks'. He also wrote a sad letter to Roger Horton at the 100 Club, which was personally upsetting, not because it mentioned me but because I could see his point. 'If you want to know the state of jazz in Britain today,' Colyer wrote, 'ask Digby Hunter Randall!'

The late Ian Hunter Randall was a marvellous, creative and high-powered trumpeter. But plainly Ian's work – and mine – failed to live up to the pure music expectations of 'the Guv'nor' and, in terms of pure New Orleans jazz, at least, he was obviously right. Ken was the first jazz musician to achieve the honour of a blue plaque (on the wall of the 100 Club), and both the Ken Colyer Foundation and Trust Band kindle the flames that he plainly believed had gone out forever. I hope he knows.

With Black Lion, Alan Bates gave me complete freedom to record for myself: a situation that allowed me to organise a session, produced by Chris Ellis, for Keith Ingham and the late Susannah McCorkle. Together we agreed a set of Johnny Mercer songs, originally assembled by Keith and Susannah for a show at the Pizza Express compèred by Peter Clayton, who had provided a typically witty title, 'The Quality of Mercer'. The resulting collection reappeared recently on the American Concord label, a memorial to Susannah's tragically terminated talents.

Meantime I was not enjoying life in Forest Gate, the down-at-heel suburb of Stratford in east London, to which Chris Watkins and I had moved. I also discovered quickly that my body clock had permanently set me to wake at seven in the morning and nothing was going to shift it.

Occasionally, though, there were relieving moments. Collecting tickets most days at Forest Gate station was an old man with furrowed brow and clenched pipe who looked remarkably like Popeye the Sailor Man. Popeye sat near a huge blackboard on which he wrote down the train cancellations, of which there were plenty. One disastrous morning, snow had fallen and the list of cancellations had worked its way right to the bottom of the board and then across the pavement. Across the board with its table of disasters, Popeye had written a simple conclusive message – 'We're up the wall!' – and abandoned ship.

Although I was no East-Ender, I was happy to be working. There were pubs which presented jazz regularly and, more modestly, the small circuit of city taverns (such as the Rumbo, close to Fleet Street) where I, as well as former stars of the trad boom, still played. These little groups often included Scottish musicians, several of whom had moved in and out of the pioneering Scottish traditional band the Clyde Valley Stompers. On one occasion, back in the late 1950s, this fine group had played in Dumfries and afterwards met with a drunken visitor in the dressing room.

'Which one's Clyde?' he enquired.

To save time, leader Pete Kerr said, 'That's me!'

'Well Mr Valley – your bloody band's duff!'

Amongst this Scottish contingent was pianist-trombonist Bert Murray. Bert had played in many fine bands during the trad boom but his sense of humour frequently led him, amid a lazy ballad improvisation, to insert some deflationary quote from 'Yes We Have No Bananas' or similar. He was also anarchically humorous in conversation, as once when a clarinet playing visitor to the Rumbo developed a reed squeak that carried on relentlessly until half-time.

'Bert,' the luckless visitor enquired. 'Have you got sixpence? I want to burn my clarinet reed.'

'Here's half a crown,' retorted Bert. 'Burn the lot!'

Another time, American guitarist Barney Kessel was playing at 100 Oxford Street and at one point stilled the room with a solo version of 'Body and Soul' into which, in the middle-eight, he had pointedly inserted a substitute chord. As the adjusted harmony sailed out into the silence of the attentive crowd it was met by a disapproving fortissimo bark from the bar. 'Wrong!' It was Bert Murray. After that, Roger Horton banned his guest from the club for a time, until, repentantly, Bert reappeared one night at the club doorway with his dog and asked the attendant to tell Roger he was there. Horton cocked his head reflectively and gave the matter some thought.

'Tell the dog he can come in,' he concluded. 'And tell Bert to go home!'

Night after night I played at regular haunts with Ron Russell or Lennie Hastings. But these once prized jobs were becoming harder to accept as my datebook filled with more prestigious work – with Keith Nichols amongst others. Thanks to Keith, I worked with his scholarly Ragtime Orchestra and in his small groups and tribute shows, regularly recording and broadcasting. This work was invariably a musical challenge and always paid well. One major priority in those early years was to make money so I seized every opportunity to play for proper returns and regularly got used to dropping in on the Forest Gate Abbey National with another thousand pounds to ward off financial insecurities.

Then, as now, Keith was one of our music's most skilled and painstaking authorities and he has a lively sense of humour, demonstrated one morning when his milkman knocked for payment. 'That'll be one seventy-eight!' said the visitor, totalling his bill. Keith darted into his music room and handed over a vintage gramophone record.

One morning, he phoned with a new project in mind. 'Digby,' he said, 'I've been to see a new show in London, 'Bubbling Brown Sugar'.' The music it celebrated was hot Harlem-style jazz of the 1920s and early 1930s and this was the first of a succession of West End reviews which would include 'One Mo' Time!' and, later, 'Five Guys Named Mo!' Its stars included Elaine Delmar and an onstage jazz group.

'It's a wonderful show!' Keith enthused. 'And I want to form a big band to play that kind of music. What do you think? Who could we get?'

Between us we hatched a list of players for a band to be called the Midnite Follies Orchestra and Keith even arranged a group visit to 'Bubbling Brown Sugar'. Most of the Midnite Men, as we became known, looked forward to our upcoming project except, to my regret, trumpeter Colin Smith who turned down the lead trumpet chair. So it was decided to ask Nick Stevenson, himself a fine lead player and jazzman who not only blew with power and accuracy but regularly let loose a sly sense of dry, often ribald humour. Nick loved Keith's idea and had already seen the show, which he promptly re-christened 'Bubbling Brown Trousers'.

All through my tenure with the Midnite Follies, Nick played lead trumpet, courageously overcoming a damaging bout of Bell's Palsy that he developed soon after the orchestra began. This resembles a minor stroke, and paralyses face muscles, so that playing the trumpet becomes a physical impossibility. Several jazz trumpeters, including the phenomenal Rod Mason – and later, me too – have suffered the illness and recovery can take years but luckily Nick was back in his trumpet chair within six weeks. With his lead, Alan Elsdon as second trumpet, and my cornet as third we made an enthusiastic trumpet section.

We were all jazz soloists too but received a mild come-uppance when, one Saturday morning, in the midst of our regular rehearsal in Grays Inn Road, Keith announced that there was a new trumpet feature ready to go. All of us looked expectantly for the word 'solo' at the top of our part but the music was handed on to bassist Bob Taylor. Bob put his part on a music-stand, produced a battered trumpet and proceeded to blow the building down with an Armstrong-esque version of 'The Sheik of Araby', bursting with unexpected power, which subsequently he performed onstage in full Egyptian rig.

For over a year the Midnite Follies showed signs of progress to 'the big time'. Our launch at the 100 Club was ecstatically reviewed in the press; the band was signed to EMI by jazz singer/philanthropist Chris Ellis and produced a single, 'No Strings', which was widely played on Radio 2, as well as a debut album 'Hotter than Hades'. In short, we were news, with radio and television spots to spare.

At one point, the orchestra was booked into the legendary Maida Vale 3 studio where Bing Crosby had made his last recordings. This was for a mammoth two-day session and a podium had been built with the trumpet section twelve feet above the ground, trombones below, then saxophones and rhythm section at ground level. One of our tunes began with a spectacular trumpet solo from Alan Elsdon but when the red light went on and conductor Alan Cohen gave the down-beat nothing was heard. Elsdon's friends in the trumpet section looked around to find a vacant space between them. Alan had fallen backwards in his chair and was twelve feet below us, unhurt, luckily, and with trumpet intact.

The title 'Midnite Follies Orchestra' had been coined earlier for a studio orchestra assembled to accompany the vocal group Sweet Substitute. Keith Nichols and Alan Cohen had both been centrally involved in their debut album, 'Something Special', which fully lived up to its title. And very soon, Sweet Substitute – Terri Leggatt, Chris Staples and Angie Masterson – were working regularly with the Follies as well as with small breakaway groups drawn from its ranks, which regularly included me. Beautiful, hard-living, and a tripartite monument to women's liberation, the Substitutes could drink most of their musician colleagues under the table, and possessed a collective and distinctly raunchy sense of humour.

In 1978, at the same time that plans for the Midnite Follies Orchestra were being laid, a new colleague, the great double-bassist Len Skeat, had introduced my name to two top session guitarists, Ike Isaacs and Denny Wright, with the idea that we might form a group together. Denny invited me to a tryout and the evening went well so we began rehearsing. Denny thought up several names for the band and then said, 'Why don't we call it Velvet? I've already made an album with a similar group using that title anyhow.'

I agreed, although privately wondered if the name was a little too fey for comfort. Dick Sudhalter thought so too. 'Maybe,' he suggested, 'you could form another group with two banjos and a tuba, and call it Horsehair!'

As an experienced session player of almost forty years, Denny had many stories to tell. One of them concerned a TV appearance on 'Come Dancing' for a decidedly snooty pair of dance champions who had given the musicians hell. Come the live transmission, Denny and his colleagues found sweet revenge. Every fourth bar they slipped in an extra beat at no extra charge.

Denny's most high-profile work was alongside Lonnie Donegan for all of his greatest hit-making years. Lonnie had played pantomime too, often in the role of 'Buttons', and for one such Christmas season Denny, whose striking facial characteristics included two devilish wrinkles rising from eyebrows to forehead at forty-five degrees, was cast in the dual role of musical director and Demon King. As Lonnie pronounced the magic word, the Demon King would appear, black-cloaked, to a chorus of horrified hisses and boos. In plenty of time for his cue, Denny would surreptitiously leave the stand and make his way to the bigger of two understage trapdoors from which he was propelled to the stage with a deafening clap of thunder to utter his menacing opening line, 'T'is well you sent for me!'

One night, in a little too much haste, Denny climbed on to the small trapdoor by mistake. Up he went, amid the clap of thunder, only to find himself stuck at shoulder level, surveying an audience mystified at this underworld visitor's inability to transport himself, head to toe, from underworld to centre stage. There was only one possible way to get over this and Denny, squinting from the stage floor, took it.

'T'is well you sent for me,' he told the mystified Donegan. 'But if you just hang on a minute, I'll be back!' And down he went again.

Velvet took off after our first appearance in 1977 and we worked together for three years. Bandleader Stan Reynolds, once one of Ted Heath's principal trumpeters, became our manager and we recorded for the Rediffusion label and Black Lion. Recording with Velvet was initially a problem for me. In a studio, our group operated with needlepoint delicacy at minimum volume and the sound of my cornet seemed to me to stick out amid the dry studio acoustics, like a handful of sore thumbs. The problem was solved by Stan Reynolds at Morgan Studios who fixed for me to record through a microphone linked up to headphones which – correctly adjusted – not only brought up the volume of my accompanists but made the cornet sound as if I were playing in a cathedral. After this, recording became less of a trial and it's a pity that the best records we made (at Morgan around 1979) were never issued.

Velvet developed a set programme which made concerts easier but introduced me, for the first time, to the challenge of keeping music fresh when re-playing it night after night.

Our tours included a week around Birmingham and the Black Country where we found ourselves in a cheap and none-too-cheerful hotel along Hagley Road. Poor Len Skeat came off worst this time. His room had an unaccountable smell of paint and we found out at the end of our stay that our hosts were surreptitiously re-decorating: while Len was out they would paint the parts of his room that he wouldn't be liable to touch including ceiling and skirting boards.

More memorably, we made the five-day 'Midlands run' which, for many British jazzmen, constituted a tour-proper back in the 1970s: Halifax on Wednesday, Burnley on Thursday, the Warren Bulkley Hotel at Stockport on Friday, Stoke-on-Trent on Saturday and ending up at Birch Hall, Oldham, on Sunday. On our tour we passed through Rochdale on the day of Gracie Fields' death: flags were visible flying at half-mast.

After a while, Velvet became less of a playing pleasure. Set behind his small Fender Stratocaster, Denny directed a non-stop volley of vivacious ideas at both audience and fellow players, making plentiful use of a tremolo arm to imitate a trumpet-section at full power and occasionally rushing the beat a little in his urgent desire to get the music across. This was a failing of mine too, causing Len Skeat visible distress. Ike, by contrast, would play with the delicacy that charac-terised his personality, sitting back smiling, holding the beat as a mother cat might enfold a favourite kitten.

Velvet was a popular group, and might have continued for longer. But gradually I realised that the creative dominance of Denny's guitar – rather like his big hearted personality – was pushing my own playing, as well as my musical thoughts, back into a corner. It was at this point in my career, too, that Len and I found for a few years that we couldn't get along. This, while it lasted, proved distressing and after a while the atmosphere on the stand became impossible. I retired for a short rest to take the weight off my tired, overstrained lip and Velvet was no more.

***

Over the next few years, life as a professional jazz musician swung from highs to lows. One of the new challenges that faced me was playing more broadcasts for the BBC 'Sounds of Jazz' radio programme which was then recorded at 7.30 in the evening, live, before a full audience. While this body of people often contained a hard core of jazz fans, at other times it was composed of casual visitors who seemed to be there mainly to keep warm.

I became a regular on BBC 'Jazz Club' compèred by Peter Clayton and a session with Bernie Cash's 'Great Jazz Solos Revisited' was particularly nerve-racking. Bernie had orchestrated a number of classic jazz solos and I was to play Armstrong's challenging 1925 outing on 'Struttin' with Some Barbecue'. This piece is a trumpeter's horror, the solo emerging straight out of an orchestrated ensemble, and it had to be accomplished in one take. That night I paced the Maida Vale corridors with more than my usual sense of foreboding and arrived on set with nothing much less than a full attack of 'the pearlies' – that feared performers' condition in which pearls of sweat break out on the player's forehead (and other less mentionable areas). Somehow, playing into a tight tin mute, I got away with the performance but it's not one I'd like to hear now.

In July 1978 – very early in my fulltime professional career – Lennie Hastings died. Britain's greatest ever dixieland drummer had walked ahead of his Alex Welsh colleagues into oblivion. A year or so before, he had suffered a mild warning stroke, after which a doctor had said, 'No more drink – or cigarettes!' But Lennie had chosen to ignore the ultimatum completely. A series of strokes ended his life and the funeral and party that followed was notable for one happy outcome, a reconciliation between John Barnes and Alex Welsh.

By 1978, other grim shadows were on the horizon. Chris had been a great support but, after a difficult time, she and I separated and, in the same year, I became aware that my father was becoming seriously ill. He had developed prostate cancer and it was spreading to his liver. Amid my non-stop schedule of work I made irregular visits home. For almost twenty years we had jousted, argued and almost fought over musical differences, sacrificing all the closeness of my pre-jazz childhood years. Yet now, just as we were mutually arriving at the conclusion that the qualities of good music in any sphere are uniform, he was succumbing visibly to a far more unanswerable challenge, the developing effects of a terminal illness from which he died in October 1979.

My father had seldom offered advice or thoughts on life but one short observation stays with me. One day, in his later years, I had asked him if it seemed as if his life had flown by, as time, for me, seemed to be passing so fast. John looked at me hard for a second. 'It's a long time,' he said, after thinking for a moment. 'You get a long time.' I never forgot the phrase but now, for my father, time had run out at last.

There didn't seem enough time to grieve, or even to think clearly about what should be done. Ena came to live with me in the tiny one bedroom flat at Forest Gate while she got over her loss and our old home was left empty. During that time it was burgled for good measure. Finally Stannetts was sold by auction for only a fraction of its estimated value.

In the days and weeks that followed this sale I realised that now there really was 'no turning back'. We had sold our shares in the 'moon country' where I had grown up. No longer could I blow my horn easily in open country with birds and cattle for company. The great echoing acoustics of our old rooms had been sold too and I would miss them for twenty more years. Life was closing doors on all sides.

Later Ena bought a new home, Rose Cottage, in the neighbouring village of Canewdon. While living there, she saw a lot of her elder brother Douglas, a man who enjoyed life to the full and, aged nearly eighty, wrote an aggrieved letter to his doctor complaining that he had been impotent for almost three weeks. Doug was also an insomniac who passed his nights composing limericks for *Playboy* and *Forum* magazines. In due course Ena challenged him to produce one for Canewdon and within ten minutes he rang her back with this:

> There was a young girl of Canewdon
> Had a poster with something quite lewd on
> With a giggle she said
> It will stand at the head
> Of the bed that I'm normally screwed on!

For a while my mother commuted between London and her new country home, until one day Derek Wood rang to tell me of a burglary and a small fire at Canewdon. Criminals had ransacked and defiled the cottage, throwing Ena's prized possessions in the village pond before setting fire to the interior. My mother slowly cleaned up her home, restoring furniture and replacing losses, before moving in to begin life once again.

Amid these new troubles, all the old interest in jazz and its heroes survived. I had continued to be fascinated by the career of Nat Gonella. But the chances of breaking the barriers around this legend and getting to meet him still seemed remote. So I'd more or less given up on the idea when, in 1978, I wrote a tiny column about him for the Pizza Express house magazine, ending with the thought that, 'perhaps some soon and sunny day we can persuade Nat once more to walk on stage somewhere that matters, just to hear our applause and receive our thanks.' To my astonishment, in June 1980, I had a reply:

> *Dear Mr. Fairweather,*
>
> *Very many thanks for your very pleasant remarks. My good friend Monty Montgomery (one time lead trumpet with my Big Band) sent me the programme. How interesting! Some good friends! I'm wishing you 'success' all the time. Monty will keep me posted.*
> *Always Swingcerely!*
> *Nat Gonella*

The thought that this master of the old years had bothered to acknowledge such a small tribute was marvellous. Then, I heard from my friend and fellow musician, Chris Walker, in Winchester. 'Well,' he said, 'we tend to keep it quiet! But

Nat Gonella in the 1930s

actually he goes most Thursdays to a pub near Gosport to sing. If I tell you where it is, will you promise not to pass the word around?'

And so, one evening, Ena and I joined a gathering of Gonella fans and friends at the Park Hotel, Alverstoke, just outside Gosport, to await the arrival of Britain's first great jazz trumpet star. And then quite suddenly, there he was, smaller than I had expected, immaculately dressed, wearing a smart box-back jacket and devoid of star-presence as he joined the company. When he made his way to the bar to say 'hello', I tried to stutter out a few words about how much he had meant to me as musician and role-model.

The legend said: 'Oh well, that's nice, mate! You'd better buy me a drink then.' Nat sang with the resident band, showing that he was still every bit the master showman he had always been. Gonella standards delighted the audience and I was invited to sit in too, experiencing the decidedly mixed emotion of blowing the cornet with my lifelong hero cocking a critical ear at my side.

5.

all roads lead to jazz

By 1978 I was getting used to the idea of touring and the phone was beginning to ring for guest-spots – a good one might pay twenty-five pounds. Such trips beyond London were usually to clubs and pubs to play one-nighters with local rhythm sections. They also offered the novelty of one or more nights in 'bed and breakfast' or 'digs' and events in many such digs became legends amongst travelling players.

One of them concerns Bruce Turner who one night had checked into digs with his Jump Band to find every room taken save for a topfloor dormitory already filled with a platoon of snoring heavy-goods lorry drivers. 'You can take mattresses on the floor in between the beds,' suggested the host. Bruce turned in immediately, grasping for sleep amid the snores and nocturnal emissions of his bedfellows above. He had dropped off into a doze when Pete Strange and John Chilton arrived, tripping over Turner's feet in the darkness. Bruce opened one bleary eye.

'Postman, Dad! Postman!'

His friends paused, mystified.

'Postman, chaps! Letter fellow get some sleep!'

At four-thirty in the morning, members of the Jump Band, including their leader, were awakened by the clangour of an enormous alarm clock heralding the tattoo of lorry drivers' feet hitting the floor in unison. One friendly giant looked down at Turner and dug him in the ribs. 'Time to go to work, mate!' Turner opened one eye.

'Not going to work, Dad! Not going to work!'

'That's right, mate,' responded his jovial assailant. 'Fuck 'em!'

The most famous digs for musicians, in its day, was 'Mrs Mac's' in Manchester where many top class players stayed. One of the regular visitors to Mrs Mac was Britain's greatest-ever tenor saxophonist Tubby Hayes, often with his quintet, and one night a monumental party ensued. Tubby, having reached the limits of self-indulgence, ran up the stairs to the toilet and burst in, delivering the contents of his stomach to what should have been the bowl of the lavatory. Unfortunately Mrs Mac was sitting there at the time.

Perhaps the most vivid and possibly apocryphal story of Mrs Mac's, however, concerns a well-known jazz pianist who came back to his lodgings after work and decided to visit the lavatory. While sitting, he smoked a comforting cigarette and afterwards dropped the butt into the pan. What he didn't know was that earlier on that day Mrs Mac had emptied the remains of a bottle of chemical cleaner into the lavatory bowl. The resulting explosion blew him off the toilet seat and out onto the landing. When ambulance men arrived with a stretcher they asked how the accident happened and, on hearing, dissolved into laughter, dropped their patient off his stretcher and broke his leg.

Few of my experiences were as devastating as that but I did have one or two surprises. In Swansea, when arriving at my digs after a long trip across country, I checked in, undressed and collapsed into bed, just in time to see a long, hairy leg pull itself hastily under my pillow. I don't like spiders and, pulling a towel round me, ran back downstairs.

'Sorry,' I gasped, 'but there's a spider in my bed. And he's enormous!'

'Oh, there's unusual,' returned my unperturbed host. 'He's normally in the sitting room!'

Some landladies over the years have become well-known on – and off – the jazz scene for 'enhanced hospitality'. On one occasion a colleague of mine, involved in a long summer season, checked in for several weeks' stay at a seaside pensionnaire and struck up a fruitful relationship with his new hostess. One afternoon he arrived back unexpectedly after a shopping trip, opened the door and met the gaze of his landlady looking backwards across the kitchen table as she was commandingly bestraddled by a fellow-member of the orchestra.

'Oh Mr B!' she protested weakly but with admirable command of understatement. 'You'll think me a terrible flirt!'

Guesting with local rhythm sections in clubs countrywide is part of the weekly touring schedule for busy jazz musicians and over the years I was lucky enough to do so regularly. One night, however, I arrived at a club in Witney to find it deserted except for three teenage boys who looked to me as if long trousers might be a relatively new adventure.

'Waiting for Mum and Dad?' I enquired.

'No,' they chorused. 'We're your rhythm section!'

'Ah,' I said, thinking fast about how to fill an evening. 'Well – can you play a blues?'

'Yes!'

'Do you know any slow tunes – ballads?'

'Yes!'

'Well, how about 'Georgia on My Mind''

'Certainly,' said one of the lads. 'What key – D-flat or F?' Nobody, anywhere in my acquaintance, knew that 'Georgia' is sometimes played (and was by Nat Gonella at one time) in D-flat. 'Well, F is fine,' I said.

'Good,' said my diminutive accompanist. 'And do you know the verse?'

Of course I did! But these were plainly no ordinary school-boys. And when we started playing, Andy Vinter and Mike Smith (later longtime pianist and drummer with the BBC Big Band) plus an equally gifted double-bassist, Dave Hage, swung their elderly visitor into the best of health.

One unusual trip came as a result of a phone call from a 'Very Famous Actress'. In a wonderfully seductive voice, the VFA enquired whether I would like to play at a party for her and several other VFAs.

This sounded like an exciting way to spend an evening. So guitarist Paul Sealey and I met the carful of VFAs at Leicester station and we drove several miles into the grounds of a large, handsome house. It was plain that this dwelling was something out of the ordinary. To begin with, there was little or no furniture and every room had been soundly, if plainly, refurbished right down to brand-new points for electricity. Upstairs there appeared to be a well-stocked library and dormitories. There was only time to look quickly but it was most obvious that the front room was furnished only with a selection of rough and ready chairs and, nearby, two gigantic trestle-tables boasting a royal banquet of food: Scottish smoked salmon, monumental sides of beef and game and salvers full of fresh strawberries.

On the stroke of eight, a doorbell rang and through the door piled a small army of men: swarthy, rowdy, decked out in overalls and leathers, and mostly drunk. Within twenty minutes all the food was gone and the new arrivals were ranged over the floor or lolling in hastily assembled hard-backed chairs. For this audience of toughs, our VFAs put on a short show of relatively austere dramatic sketches, which were given the ungracious bird. To finish the evening, we were invited to play for a sing-song which was at least lively – until our army of guests made their exit as gracelessly fast as they had come. We repacked our instruments and with our new friends made the slow trip back through heavy snow to London.

Three weeks later, it was reported in the national press that an arms cache of considerable size had been discovered in the grounds of our one-night venue. It seems we had been playing for a private army. I wouldn't have cared to have met any of them on any other dark night.

***

After touring had become a regular part of my datesheet, I met a man who for ten years would become my closest friend in the music world: the Lancashire-based pianist Stan Barker. The first time we met was a strange day. During the late 1970s it was still much cheaper to travel across country by coach than by rail. Booked with Pete Strange to play a double guest-spot at Kendal Arts Centre in Cumbria, I decided to introduce Pete to my new way of travelling.

'Come on,' I said. 'Let's do it by coach!'

'Erf, erf,' said Pete, locked into Bruce Turner mode. 'Don't know really! Don't know really! Coaches crash, don't they?'

'Never,' I said firmly. 'Never in my experience!'

And against my friend's wishes, we booked seats. Once out of Victoria Coach Station, we dozed safely on the motorway but then, quite suddenly, I woke to the sound of metal tearing and saw a lorry to our left colliding, apparently in slow motion, with our coach as it sped along the outside lane of the motorway. There was a crash as its bodywork shattered our windows and people screamed as we rode up onto the central reservation and ground to a halt. From behind came a heavy and conclusive thud as a car collided with us from behind.

'Told you, told you!' said Pete when we'd both stopped shaking.

Eventually a second coach arrived to take the passengers on to Kendal. On arrival, Pete and I disembarked and made our way into the club to be greeted by a bright-eyed bearded man of about fifty with a beaming smile. 'Welcome,' said the new arrival. 'I'm Stan Barker! What do you think we should play tonight?'

At the piano, my new acquaintance combined attacking right-hand figures in the Errol Garner/Oscar Peterson mould with fully-chorded ballad explorations bringing to mind Bill Evans. He knew every tune we called and his playing fitted easily into the kind of swing-based approach that Pete and I were looking for. The evening was an unqualified success and a few days later Stan rang up. Would I, he asked, play a guest spot with him at Blackpool's long running jazz club at Raikes Hall.

'You're welcome to stay with me of course. Come back to Clitheroe and we'll share a drink afterwards if you'd like.'

Blackpool was a similarly joyful event and we had time to talk. Stan, like me, had turned professional late on, in his case at the age of fifty-two, but the world of the jobbing jazz musician was already troubling him. Naturally aware of life's courtesies, he hated the casual labour aspect of the lifestyle: pound notes counted into his hand in public at the end of the night, over-familiarity from people who believed that because they had hired him they owned him. I, too, had become unhappy in the hurly-burly of my new regime and was at one with Stan in my feelings about the professional jazz life.

'I've been wondering,' said Stan, 'if there mightn't be some possibility of us teaching jazz, instead of just playing it. Wouldn't that be a worthwhile thing? And I've met a man, James Platt, who runs the Central Bureau for Cultural Visits and Exchange down in Baker Street in London. He's very interested in the idea and might be able to help. Would you like to go and see him with me?'

'Of course I would.'

With James Platt, we laid the foundations of a new educational project which we called 'Jazz College'. Our organisation was to be registered as a non-profit-making trust and our mission – as well as our slogan on specially designed notepaper – was to bring 'the art of improvisation into the school curriculum'. Never averse to a celebration in a worthy cause, James also decided that we should have both a southern and a northern launch. The southern end, at his offices in Baker Street, involved a classy lunchtime party and jam-session in which the newly assembled Jazz College Quintet (Danny Moss, Spike Heatley, Derek Hogg, Stan and I) was joined unobtrusively by Louis Bellson who tiptoed to the drum stool to play brushes for a tune or two. And at our northern launch at Raikes Hall Jazz Club, Blackpool, we proudly and rather drunkenly announced ourselves to a small audience who may have noticed that these pioneer educators were, to say the least, a bit merry.

The Jazz College Quintet was a little too large – and expensive – for longterm teaching activities. But it was a marvellous group and on one occasion Stan's sense of humour found a focus with bassist Spike Heatley. 'The concert,' Stan explained, 'is in Burnley. Perhaps you and Digby could travel up together?'

'Good idea,' said Spike. 'Give me Digby's number and I'll write it in my book.'

'OK,' said Stan carefully. 'It's 01- '

'01.....'

'2-3-4'

'2-3-4'

'5-6-7-8....'

'5-6-7-8.....'

'9-10-11....' Stan continued wickedly.

'You stupid bastard! I've written that in my book now!'

As Stan took hold of his new project, work burgeoned. First we visited small schools in the Lancashire area, finding our feet and tussling with the difficulties of trying to explain the processes behind what, so far, we had done naturally. Gentle, sophisticated, deeply sensitive and too intelligent for his new surroundings, Stan also knew how to laugh at the more philistine aspects of playing jazz for a living.

'Yes,' he would begin, with a semi-maniacal gleam. 'It's all true. See them in the front row smoking their big cigars! They're saying, "By gum! Look at that Digby! He doesn't half go red when he plays! He's bound for a stroke to be sure." Go on Digby! Blow and die!'

'Blow and die!' I echoed. The phrase became a frequent litany.

Stan had his own well thought-out set of defences to assaults from beyond his circle. On one occasion, I saw him cornered at the bar by someone who insisted on explaining why Stan hadn't played so well this night as he had previously. Forefingers to his lips, quizzical humorous eyes focussed on his assailant Stan listened to the very end, and then leaned across.

'Well, it's funny that you should have been so observant,' he returned. 'But it's very good too, you know! Because an artist, if that's what he chooses to call himself, has a job night by night. Too close to the performance, you see, and sometimes it's possible to lose track of the creative threads that make for maximum effect.' The listener leaned forwards fascinated, as Stan warmed to his theme.

'So,' Stan continued, 'in a sense we are beholden to our listeners. Beholden to their judgment and objective sense of what's right and wrong, what works and what doesn't. For the artist it's often a case of hopeless hit and miss, only to be monitored by the objective view of people like yourself. So I must tell you that I'm grateful for your views.'

'You cunt,' he added as his delighted interrogator turned away. Stan swore very selectively – when deeply aggravated he used either 'cunting twathooks!' or, equally remarkably, 'shag a donkey!' and never in the wrong company. Once, driving to a gig, I told him a funny but very vulgar story. Stan laughed and then looked reflective for a moment.

'What are you thinking?' I asked.

'It just occurred to me,' said Stan, 'that we're laughing. But young people might just look at us and say, "What a pair of dirty old men!"' And in many ways he was right. It was no longer the sixties when anything used to go: a new prurience was in the air.

While he had ironed out every regional inflection from his well-modulated voice, Stan was ready at any point to re-assume an accent of loony Lancastrian proportions. And with such simple defences, for the time being, we kept at bay the worst aspects of the cartoon world we'd both chosen to inhabit. Working in schools or arts centres we would once again see something of the sort of people we'd lost contact with. And we would meet them on terms that, for now, were more congenial for us than the smoky world of nightclubs and their shadowy inhabitants.

Our initial efforts to teach jazz were not always easy, nor faultless, but a good day's work was highly rewarding. Faced with anything, from a primary school group armed with glockenspiels and recorders to groups of teenagers wearing Iron Maiden tee-shirts and toting flat guitars, we doggedly tried to teach improvisation, learning as we went along. Stan's obvious sincerity endeared our project to all who came into contact with him and we were offered the posts of 'artists in residence' at Southport Arts Centre. We also began travelling to local schools and taught at the Arts Centre in the evening for good measure.

Like many others, I benefited from Stan's good nature. Several times, particularly after we worked together less, a cheque would arrive. 'From our joint account,' explained the accompanying note, 'following the sale of tapes.' I had seldom been aware of such sales. Stan was also involved in charitable activities but they were always discreet and his one mention of them that I can remember was typically self-deflationary. Sometime before we met he had visited a near-by mental hospital where in due course he had done his best to befriend a lonely silent inmate.

'I thought I was doing quite nicely,' Stan said. 'To begin with he just stared silently and straight ahead. Then one day he turned to look at me when I arrived. Then a few weeks later we walked around the room together. And then I took in a football and we kicked it around. And I knew that one day soon he was going to speak to me. And finally, after all those weeks, he did!'

'What did he say?' I asked.

Stan burst into ready laughter. 'He said, "Oh why don't you fuck off and leave me alone!"'

Stan enjoyed the bathetic aspect of that story. Inside him lurked a man dogged by personal insecurity who went out of his way, as I did, to project an image of ready bonhomie but for whom – like me again – the constant companionship of the world could occasionally turn into a damaging strain. When this happened Stan would say, 'I'm going out to smoke my pipe,' taking comfort from the promise of five minutes release from the social demands of the world.

At the same time as I was getting to know Stan Barker, I carried on working in London. Peter Boizot included me in the Pizza Express All-stars, a newly formed house band for his club at 10 Dean Street. This consisted of invited premier mainstream players including Danny Moss, Dave Shepherd, Roy Williams, Brian Lemon, Len Skeat and Kenny Clare. We were to play every Tuesday, there was to be an album (on Peter's Pizza label) and we were to launch the project as part of an all-day jazz festival at the Bloomsbury Hotel. I arrived to find, at one window of the hotel, an enormous double life-size portrait of me, haloed with hair in full flight, a study by Tim Motian which I used as an effective publicity shot for several years.

Jazz legends dropped into the Pizza Express on a nightly basis. American promoter Ernie Anderson, who masterminded everything from Eddie Condon's 1940s broadcasts to Louis Armstrong's All Stars, regularly sat at the back of the room to listen and hold court. Tony Bennett would quietly slip into an alcove seat on occasion and so, from time to time, did Princess Margaret with her entourage. Slim Gaillard – looking like a benevolent, streamlined Uncle Remus – would arrive bearing his huge scrapbook of cuttings for all to view. And smaller legends dropped in to London's mainstream Mecca too, amongst them Heinie Beau, longtime sideman to the great cornetist Red Nichols. Heinie personified gentle charm and, when he discovered my adoration of Nichols, brought a handwritten composition for me as a present.

One regular member of our audience was cricketer and MCC official Doug Insole. I know nothing about cricket but remembered Doug from early years when he played for Essex. One night he came in with a friend.

'Hello, Doug,' I said. 'How are things in the cricket world?'

'Fine. And this is Bob Willis.'

'Good to meet you,' I said. 'And are you involved in cricket at all?' Willis was captain of England at the time.

One of the most diverting experiences in the Pizza All-stars was the chance to work with the phenomenal drummer

Kenny Clare. I remembered him on Billy Cotton's television specials playing blistering duets with trumpeter Grisha Farfel and later with Buddy Rich. Kenny went out of his way to be friendly. On one occasion we were sharing the stand with Ruby Braff and Ruby drew me into a duet. I played as well as I could and afterwards Kenny bothered to take my arm. 'That was great,' he said, 'and you played really nicely. Well done!'

The Pizza All-stars were regularly teamed with American guests including the formidable singer Jimmy Witherspoon. One of Jimmy's blues was economically titled 'Don't gotta!'

'Don't gotta go to the dentist in the morning
'cos I'm gonna knock out all your teeth tonight!'

The musicians all around me were super but I was going through a phase when my playing wasn't as good as it might have been and the acoustics at the Pizza Express were far from encouraging. As a result, I frequently depped the job and there was one band member who battened unmercifully on my shortcomings. The situation began to feel like war, and despite the fact that I knew I wasn't always playing as well as I could, I fought back, refusing to be hoisted out of the group until I was good and ready. Eventually I left and for a couple of years afterwards my rival and I continued our sparring match. But in the end we forgot our differences: the jazz world is too small for quarrels.

At this time, I first visited the veteran Scots trumpeter Tommy McQuater at his Ealing home. Tommy is generally recognised as the greatest British trumpet teacher in his field.

'What would a lesson cost?' I had asked cautiously.

'I drink Black Label,' said Tommy cheerfully.

At our first meeting, Tommy showed me exercises which both relaxed my lip and reconstructed my trumpet embouchure. His only payment, as agreed, was a bottle of Black Label whisky, left on the sitting room table before the lesson began.

Thomas Mossie McQuater made his name in the 1930s working with Jack Payne, then replaced Nat Gonella in Lew

Stone's orchestra in 1935 and later went on to play lead in the Squadronaires. He is one of the music profession's strongest and most respected players and his booming voice – easily projected across any orchestra pit – was a regular source of now legendary one-liners. One of these was directed at young Tom Jones who – just arrived at the height of stardom – was due to rehearse with the Jack Parnell Orchestra at ten o'clock one morning. One and a quarter hours later, the newly established superstar singer wandered casually in, unconcerned at having kept ranks of professional colleagues waiting for no good reason. From the trumpet section Tommy McQuater's bark was clearly heard, 'I suppose a bollocking's out of the question?'

By the time I knew him, Tommy was semi-retired after an onstage accident which severely damaged his lip. A trumpet partner had completed a vocal routine with an extravagant arm gesture which accidentally hit the bell of Tommy's trumpet, driving the mouthpiece through his lip and teeth, and causing severe damage in the process. Now he was working his way back to performance after extensive dental treatment and the regular intake of whisky and his love of good music showed every sign of carrying him, like bandleader Harry Gold, into old age and better health than ever.

At around this time, Tommy had heard the young Wynton Marsalis at Ronnie Scott's, found himself impressed, and introduced himself. 'Would you like to come home and have a whisky or two?'

'I don't drink,' said Marsalis. Tommy considered this extraordinary situation for a moment.

'Well,' he said, 'would you like to come back home, and I'll have my wife cook us a fine big steak?'

'I'm a vegetarian!' responded Marsalis. Tommy was only temporarily at a loss.

'Well,' he said, 'let's go back home to my place. And you can have a wee nibble at my hedge!'

***

While I was working with the Pizza Express All-stars in the late 1970s, we took part in a spectacular set of one-night jazz festivals at a large college in Barking for promoter Ken Lodge and one night the star guest was Billy Butterfield. I opened the show with pianist Fred Hunt, and Kenny Baker, who followed, turned his own set into a tribute to Billy, playing a number of his hit tunes including 'Alfie' and 'What's New'. Billy came over to the bar, looking worried.

'This guy's playing all my tunes,' he muttered. 'What am I going to do?'

'Whatever you play,' I said with absolute sincerity, 'we all know it's going to be wonderful. Will you have a drink with me?'

Billy accepted a triple vodka and made his way back through the crowd. Naturally, I supposed, that would be the last I saw of him. But later that night I saw this great trumpeter across the room packed with sixty musicians. Billy saw me and caught my eye with a nod. Then lifting a full bottle of vodka to a tumbler he ceremoniously poured a generous three fingers and with difficulty made his way through the teeming crowd to hand me the glass with a smile.

I never got to know Billy well, but much later on I heard him again at Pizza Express with Brian Lemon's Trio. On Hoagy Carmichael's 'New Orleans', he told a musical story over three choruses with the skill of a musical Hans Christian Andersen, moving from point to point until at the peak of his solo, a natural climax, the crowd, rather than applauding, actually screamed with pleasure! His regular attacks on the upper register were like rocket-flares that illuminated the solo and then fell gracefully. And sometimes the vulnerable effect of a fall at the end of a note recalled a wistful sigh.

One American giant I got to know better than most was cornetist Wild Bill Davison. Wild Bill had been an idol ever since I'd read the pen portrait of him in Eddie Condon's *Treasury of Jazz*: a hard-blowing, ribald young man from Defiance, Ohio, who – it was said – once stunned a turkey by blowing a shattering top C in its ear on the road home. From the mid-1960s Bill worked regularly in Europe where for twenty or more years he maintained a huge reputation as a solo performer.

As a cornetist, Wild Bill was once dismissed as a less subtle copy of Louis Armstrong but – far from that! – he was a divinely original alternative. The record that introduced me to him back in 1961 was the superb 'Pretty Wild' with Percy Faith's strings and in the mid-1970s I played opposite Bill with the Alex Welsh Band. Never have I heard such power issue from a cornet. Some indication of the strength and wild, free creativity of Bill at his height with Alex's band can still be heard on the album 'Blowin' Wild' but you can also hear exquisite tenderness in there too.

Wild Bill was reminiscing one day. 'Yeah!' he said, leaning forward, wide-eyed, fingering the valves of his King cornet. 'You know, when I was young we'd all get together back down in Ohio, round the pot-bellied stove. And we'd play cracker-barrel music! Yeah – that's what we called it – crackerbarrel music. Sounded good!'

I loved the phrase and wrote a little tune using it as a title. The next time I saw Bill I showed him the music and his eyes widened.

'So,' he said uncomprehendingly, 'what the hell is cracker-barrel music?'

In 1979 Bill came to do a guest spot with the Midnight Follies Orchestra at the Canteen Club in Holborn. A dedicated and professional performer, he practised every day to his own records and always left copious time for a 'warm-up' prior to the job. Most trumpet players use a warm-up routine: the process involves gentle huffs through the instrument, gradual production of one or two notes and then scientifically extended exercises, until the top of the trumpet-range of notes can be produced easily. In other words, the lip is gradually warmed up for the night's work to avoid the lip strain that can otherwise follow. On this occasion I accompanied Bill to Holborn, presumably for his customary warm-up, two

Wild Bill Davison

hours before he was due to start work. But, in the absence of a dressing room, he installed himself upstairs at a hastily-supplied table with hipflask and glass, his cornet close by. Then for two hours he regaled us with endless stories of Eddie Condon, Pee Wee Russell and his own remarkable life until finally, at five to eight, he heard the Midnite Follies Orchestra – minus their own third cornetist, me – tuning up, ready to launch into their opener.

'OK,' said Bill. 'Time to go to work.'

Whereupon he filled his tumbler full of whisky, emptied it with relish at a gulp and lifted the cornet to his lips. One mighty blast on top C almost tore the paper off the walls of the Canteen's upper room and Wild Bill Davison, ready for work and miraculously fully warmed-up, made his relaxed way down to the bandstand.

I met Bill regularly over the years with his devoted wife, the actress Anne Stewart. The last time I saw the two of them together was in the unlikely surroundings of Butlin's Holiday Camp, Bognor Regis, for a jazz festival. The Wild One had been booked into one of the wooden boxes which, at the time, served as a standard campers' chalet. The chalets held no more than a bed and rickety cupboard, encouraging occupants either to use the room for functional veniality or to get out as soon as possible in search of the rides, bingo and on-site cinema. Bill, however, wanted to rest up in comfort before his gig and following a justified outburst he and Anne were relocated to a staff chalet with carpets, wallpaper and even a television. The only problem was that the TV, along with the bed, filled the room and when I finally re-located Bill in his new home he was sitting up in the bed, still in his bowler-hat and overcoat, looking cross.

'Goddamn it, Digby! This is the only room I've been in where you can lie in bed and take a piss in the bathroom at the same time!'

From the summer of 1979, Pete Strange and I collaborated in a group called, perhaps inevitably, Fairweather Friends, and every Thursday we played at The Prince of Wales, Buckhurst Hill. Among the Friends, drummer Tony Allen had his bass drum decorated with a metal sign he'd found on a launderette washing-machine: *Never reach into drum while spinning* it read. Pete assembled a bookful of arrangements which included, at my suggestion, tunes that strayed from the standard repertoire of dixieland groups: for example, the marvellous but difficult 'One' from the musical 'A Chorus Line', Barry Manilow's 'Copa Cabana' and more.

In a slightly later incarnation, Fairweather Friends also played BBC 'Sounds of Jazz' broadcasts in 1980 and 1981, recorded live with Peter Clayton compering. At the time of these broadcasts Pete was preoccupied with anagrams and supplied Peter Clayton with one for every band member: the fine clarinettist Randolph Colville became 'Lord Alvin Claphole', I turned into the 'Big Wet Hairy Fader' and Pete Strange himself was inelegantly transformed into 'Tent Peg

Arse'. Peter Clayton, who delighted in the tricks the English language can get up to, included all the anagrams before signing off the show with, 'So that's it for tonight's 'Sounds of Jazz' from Fairweather Friends and yours truly, 'Potty Cleaner'!'

Fairweather Friends toured Germany and played at the Northsea Jazz Festival and a bootleg album of our show was issued in 2002. On the morning after our Northsea concert, the phone rang in my hotel room and, to my surprise, it was the great American bassist, Milt 'Judge' Hinton.

'I heard part of your set, Digby,' said the Judge, 'and I'd really appreciate the chance to play with you. Could you come to my hotel room pretty soon?'

I couldn't believe my luck and raced along the hotel corridors with my cornet. There, in his room was my new admirer. 'Digby,' he said, 'when I heard you, you reminded me of the young Dizzy Gillespie – Dizzy, my friend, from Cab Calloway's band. Of course you know Dizzy? How about we should play a little blues together?'

So we did, at the conclusion of which Milt laid his bass down and posed for a photograph. 'That was really great!' he said. 'And so good to meet you Digby, my friend! I hope we'll meet up again! Oh and by the way. Over by the door you'll see my wife Monah – she has one or two things for sale. Tee-shirts! Oh and my new book! Maybe you'd like to take a look on the way out?' Laden with a purchase or two I made my way from the room – to see a fresh faced young clarinettist from a local traditional band flushed with pride and heading for the wise old Judge's room, case in hand!

I didn't meet Milt again for many years until in 1997 he was one of our interviewees when BBC 'Jazznotes' went to New York for a week. By then he had suffered a small stroke but still talked with vivid recall of his starry career as one of the central and very best loved figures in American jazz history.

Another new colleague at this time was composer-arranger and talented reedman John Altman who regularly booked me for studio sessions. John (whose uncles included clarinet-tist Sid Phillips and trombonist Woolf Phillips) now has thousands of television commercials to his credit as well as full-scale film scores. But at that time he was just starting to create a stir with his informed versatility as an arranger. We made one successful album with Dr John, called 'Such a Night', dubbing horns, keyboards (Chas Jankel) percussion and voices on to a concert recording which had been sent over by the good doctor from New Orleans. And we also spent three and a half days recording a nostalgic album for singer Robin Sarstedt called 'You Must Remember This'. On the third day, when work was over, I asked John what was involved for next morning. 'Oh nothing much,' he said, 'I think it's all very easy.'

So, later that day, I took myself with cornet to the 100 Club for a benefit which ended late with a riotous jam session including Humphrey Lyttelton and myself. Conscious of an ease-up in pressure, I drank too much and ended up in Forest Gate, confined to bathroom quarters in the small hours. Next morning I arrived at the studios with a monstrous hangover, dehydrated and with the shakes. Still things should be easy enough, as John had said. So what was this? Two chairs, one for guitarist Mitch Dalton and one for me and, screened off behind glass, thirty string players looking censorious.

'I'm sorry,' said John, 'I forgot to mention. We're doing the Gershwin ballad, 'I've Got a Crush on You', just you and Mitch and the strings. And I thought it would be nice if you played the verse alone with Mitch! Here's the music. I'll conduct you. Just try and be Bobby Hackett.'

The result is not a record I like to hear. Afterwards, in the bar, the lead violinist came over to join me.

'I used to play trumpet too,' he said.

'Why did you give up?' I asked.

'Because I had an embouchure that was worse than yours!'

John Altman and I put on a couple of shows at Pizza Express and one night John appeared in the audience – with Van Morrison. I made the mistake of asking for applause for the eminent visitor and when I looked across he was already up the stairs and away! With John's big band, I also played for two editions of the Amnesty International show, 'The Secret Policeman's Ball'. These extraordinary shows featured many of our greatest popular legends: Rowan Atkinson, John Cleese and the Monty Python team, 'Dame Edna Everidge', Pete Townsend, John Williams and Sting – just approaching the height of his fame – who sang 'Roxanne', filling the entire theatre with his huge voice. I had hardly heard of him at this point, but remember the frisson of excitement amongst the backing singers when they heard that he was coming in. The climax of the show came when Sting, backed by the Altman band, sang a powerful version of Bob Dylan's 'I Shall Be Released'.

At this time in London I regularly ran into Ruby Braff and his one-time protégé, Warren Vaché Junior, another great American cornetist. Ruby was playing – then as now – the most perfectly sculpted lyric cornet to be heard in jazz. He was also, as befits a great artist, rightly particular about the musical company he kept – and justifiably furious when mis-informed booking agents matched him with insensitive henchmen. Early on, these included a well-rated British pianist whose solo playing had rightfully earned him exposure on his own albums and a reputation larger than most of his fellows. A less than ideal accompanist nevertheless, he creat-ed mental distractions for the soloist out front and this led to conflicts off-stage and at least one in public too.

'On piano,' Ruby announced to one packed house, 'they've given me this disease!' His accompanist, who hadn't been lis-tening anyhow, nodded compliantly, savouring what he thought was adulatory applause.

It happened with Eddie Thompson too, a magnificent piano soloist and leader of his own trio. Eddie sometimes saw accompanying as more of a spirited, witty musical exchange than compliant subservience. As Ruby would bring forth some ravishing musical phrase Eddie was capable of playing it

Ruby Braff

back at him a bar or so later, then turning the idea upside down (as well as playing it backwards for good measure), disrupting the lyric flow of Braff's improvisation. Ruby exploded about this as well and a spirited correspondence ensued between the two of them.

'All I need from an accompanist is piano tenths – you know, stride piano – like Count Basie played,' Ruby explained to me one afternoon, opening the piano lid to demonstrate. I'd visited Dean Street in search of a cornet masterclass with my idol and, as always, he was constructive and friendly. 'I like the way you play,' he told me, after listening to some nervous demonstrations, and spent a long time talking about approaches to performance and the challenges involved. Six or seven years of playing jazz full time had considerably modified my ability to play classical studies as opposed to improvised choruses and Ruby opened up the standard trumpeter's study book (by Philippe Arban) which I'd taken with me.

'I can't play that shit either!' he said, generously demonstrating with what sounded like some tentative notes. 'The secret is to find out how you play, Digby – and then stick to that!'

This was some of the most valuable advice I had received until then. Later, I realised that other important cornetists said the same, notably Wild Bill Davison who practised religiously every day, but always to his own records rather than from exercise books.

As an artistic grand-master is entitled to be, Ruby was direct in expressing his views, and there were subjects it was wise to avoid. One of these was the trumpeter Max Kaminsky, as my good friend the critic and author Steve Voce found out one night at the start of a series of radio interviews for his long-running show on BBC Radio Merseyside.

'Max Kaminsky comes from Boston too, doesn't he, Ruby?' Steve had offered in the way of small talk.

'I've nothing to say about Max Kaminsky at all,' responded Ruby, leaving his discomfited interviewer to re-start the conversation with his normal skill.

Another fan fell foul of this conversational pothole. Ruby Braff's London seasons at the Pizza Express in Dean Street were frequent and luxuriously long. Night by night, this admirer sat in the club savouring the music, until Ruby gradually became aware of the regular visitor and would sometimes offer a brief, 'Good evening,' on the way back to the dressing room. The dialogue developed until Ruby was stopping at the table to share a convivial glass and one night his new friend finally spotted the right moment to offer a friendly invitation. 'Ruby! Would you like to join me later for a Courvoisier at home?'

'Sure,' agreed Ruby compliantly.

At one in the morning, the club closed and the two of them went to a luxurious apartment nearby. 'May I take your hat and coat?' the host asked, 'and please do make yourself comfortable.' Then, passing his music centre en route for a well-stocked drinks cabinet, he flipped a switch and the sound of Eddie Condon's band sprung from the speakers.

'Max Kaminsky's a good player, isn't he, Ruby?' he offered conversationally.

'Goodnight,' said Ruby and, retrieving his hat and coat, he was gone.

During our own meetings I never rubbed up against Ruby's reportedly volatile side and our conversations ranged far and wide but often returned to his inspiration, Louis Armstrong, and his close friend, Judy Garland. In the 1970s we exchanged letters and in one he advised, 'Get down to the Pizza Express and see Warren Vaché Junior. He's there now – and he's a good kid.' Soon after, I bought Warren's debut album 'First Time Out' and discovered a lyric cornetist with a style all of his own and an assurance which belied his youth. So I went to hear him and was duly knocked out within eight bars. Warren Vaché is a master of the cornet.

Over the years we would see each other at clubs and festivals and we've played together on several enjoyable occasions. One was at Clitheroe, with Stan Barker, where Warren arrived with his right hand bandaged after a severe accident. While washing up at home he'd reached for a glass at the bottom of a bowl of hot water: the glass had split and severed tendons in his left hand. Rather than cancelling his tour, Warren had a cornet re-designed so that he could play one-handed, which he did, blowing every room away in the process.

6.

music with friends

In the early 1980s, I had the chance to work on some interesting new projects and to meet some outstanding veterans of the British jazz scene. One of the first of these opportunities came in 1981 when trumpeter Joe Brickell telephoned from Bath. Joe led a band called the Swing Stars at the Redcar Hotel and over the years had had many of the same affectionate thoughts about Nat Gonella as I had.

'Digby, Why don't we do a tribute to Nat and the Georgians? Round up as many of the originals as you can and we'll put on a celebration night at the Redcar!'

It was over forty years since the Georgians' career had been brought to a halt by the war. I made exploratory phone calls one evening and the first to respond was Tiny Winters who had played bass for Nat while the Georgians were still part of Lew Stone's orchestra. 'Of course I'll come,' said Tiny immediately. Next to accept was South African Pat Smuts, Nat's longtime tenor player with the Georgians. Albert Torrance, the alto saxophonist who'd recorded with Nat in his formative years, reluctantly declined. 'I'm rather busy in the shop,' said Albert, who at the time still ran an electrical store in the Edgware Road. Harold 'Babe' Hood, the spectacular pianist who had worked with the Georgians through all their great-est years, was too ill to join us.

Nevertheless, we had a fine time at the Redcar Hotel in Bath that Sunday night. After a warm-up set from the Swing Stars – with Joe Brickell immaculately attired, playing trum-pet and singing to a background of neat arrangements – Tiny, Pat and I joined their rhythm section. Pat Smuts blew strong-ly, his pawky sound as much like late Lester Young as Coleman Hawkins.

But star of the show was Tiny Winters. On arrival, I popped my head around the door of his hotel room to find him, spruce as a nut, sitting up in bed, taking a rest after his drive. Once on the stand, he pushed the rhythm section of Joe Brickell's band along with the relentless thrust of an on-form Pops Foster. Born in Hackney in 1909, Tiny had taken up the bass at the inspiration of Spike Hughes as well as Foster and worked thereafter with every one of the top bands of the 1930s. After the war, he had gone on to become a successful session man and, at the time we met, was still leading his own Palm Court Trio at the National Theatre. From then on we got together regularly, on one later occasion to visit Nat Gonella himself at Gosport, and later collaborated on his autobiography – appropriately titled *It Took a Lot of Pluck*!

Soon after, Jazz Services offered our Nat Gonella Tribute the chance to tour nationwide and we set off for a string of dates around Britain. Our tour climaxed with a sensational evening at Gosport Jazz Club, in which Nat joined us on stage to sing along with everything. I was sure that we ought to take the idea further but, for now, Nat was busy nursing his wife Dorothy who, over the next ten years, would gradually become bed-ridden.

After our Gonella tour, Tiny and I decided to re-form the Kettners Five, a group that Tiny remembered hearing on his crystal set in the late 1920s, broadcasting live from Kettners elegant Soho restaurant. Swing violinist Hugh Rignold had led the band back then and for our new project we were joined by Tiny's close friend from his Palm Court Trio, Laurie

Rossi, who for many years played for Victor Sylvester but who also knew how to play swinging jazz choruses. Keith Nichols, John Barnes, Paul Sealey, John Armatage and singers Chris Ellis and Liza Lincoln, my friend and confidante of over twenty years, also joined us in the project. I wrote a bookful of arrangements and we both broadcast and played regularly at Dean Street though never, for some reason, at Kettners' Restaurant itself.

Over our years together I met and worked with players from Tiny's own groups. These were 'gig-men', weathered veterans in the main, who had acquired their skills in the dance-band days and now made a living through 'functions'. Amongst them were tenorist John Holbrook and Harry Conn, the craftsman altoist who had played lead for the Skyrockets, and Tiny would regularly corral a team of them to play for weddings, at golf clubs or wherever music was required.

Tiny loved seafood and on one occasion we dropped into a restaurant called the Wong Kei and ordered what Nat Gonella would have called a 'worrying' meal including soup with fish heads regularly floating to the surface of our bowls to glower at us resentfully. Tiny, however, couldn't stop laughing. 'What do you expect when you're in the Wong Key?' he gurgled. We continued to collaborate for several years until my old friend gave us all a surprise. He had re-met a girl-friend, Lillian, from his teenage years and after proper courtship, decided to remarry. Tiny Winters finally settled for a quiet life and slowed down happily until his death in 1995. I was proud to give his eulogy at Golders Green Crematorium and miss him still. But his celebrated portrait (by Sallon), donated by his widow Lillian, hangs now in the National Jazz Archive at Loughton, just where it belongs.

In the spring of 1982, Alastair Robertson of Hep Records asked if I would I like to record my 'Songs for Sandy'. This modest suite, dedicated to clarinettist Sandy Brown, had been commissioned half a dozen years earlier by the Eastern

Arts organisation and written during my first cruise with Ron Russell (pianist Barney Bates, a longtime colleague of Sandy's, had looked over the work and approved).

By now, though, I was doubtful. 'Songs for Sandy' had been played and toured and felt stale – as well as skimpy. Alastair, however, refreshed it musically for the recording with the addition of Alan Cooper, a magnificent clarinettist whose originality and jazz feeling were comparable to Sandy's own, as well as trumpeter Al Fairweather, Sandy's longtime partner in the Fairweather-Brown All Stars. I wasn't enjoying playing or recording at this point and didn't listen to the record until it came out on CD twenty years later. When I did, the 'sound of surprise' had had time to return a little and I could enjoy the music again, including featured soloist John Barnes' magnificent re-creation of Sandy's sound.

Soon after, Alastair invited me to make an album with the singer and guitarist Slim Gaillard. I turned up at Peter Ind's Wave Studio to join an all-star group and while we were waiting for Slim, Peter told us ruefully about his experience recording a punk rock group.

'The bass was just unbelievably out of tune,' he said, 'so finally I went out of the box and suggested the bass player might do something about it. When I got a blank look I took his bass and tried to do the job but the machine-heads – the tuning-pegs for the strings – wouldn't move! This lad's dad had brought him the bass and had the shop tune it up. Then he had the heads welded – so that the bass would stay in tune for ever!'

When Slim arrived, we recorded quickly, including a lengthy re-make of 'Slim's Jam' (the blues he'd originally recorded with Dizzy Gillespie and Charlie Parker) and a marvellous song he had composed called 'Everything is OK in the UK' which he had put together using a library gazetteer. It was a hip travelogue around Britain, set to a catchy, contemporary Latin beat, and though I don't do much but play backings the record is still one of my own favourites.

***

By the early 1980s Alex Welsh was well on the way to reaping the grim reward of unlimited vodka. One day I visited his new home in Ruislip to find him pale and shrunken, sitting deep in a chair and reluctantly sipping water. I had taken a present with me, a silver King cornet – the Wild Bill Davison model that he loved to play – brand-new and untouched in its case. 'I thought you might like this. It might be an encouragement to get back to blowing.'

'That's kind of you, lad,' said Alex, 'but I'm not sure.'

There was a pause and together we glanced at a table nearby on which stood a battered copy of the LP record of his Dresden concert, his classic. Alex nodded towards it.

'We had a good band,' he said, preoccupied, as if glancing back to a chapter that was closed forever. But shortly before he died Alex went back to bandleading again. There were disturbing stories of non-existent bookings, sudden cancellations, and – from Roger Horton – of a last gig at the 100 Club when Alex was plainly ill on the stand and not able to play his cornet much at all.

My own last sight of my friend and supporter was at a recording of 'Jazz Score', producer Richard Willcox's wonderful panel game which ran for nineteen years on Radio 2. This show was to be recorded, as usual, at the BBC's Paris studios in Lower Regent Street and, when he arrived, Alex was walking on crutches. Once announced onstage, however, he made a show-stopping entry. One crutch held high in his left hand became a cane while his right hand doffed an imaginary topper to the crowd. For a few seconds, Broadway Alex was back in town.

On the show, we made up a team and Alex whispered, 'Let's see if we can beat Humphrey Lyttelton!' But we didn't beat Humph and with cheerful resignation Alex waved goodbye to me as he determinedly made his lonely way, on crutches, up Lower Regent Street.

Weeks later the news came through the wires. Alex's doctor had said, 'Drink one more bottle of vodka, and that will be it.' Alex, so it was said, locked his bedroom door and drank his

Fred Hunt

way into the next world. His funeral in 1982 was packed and, with grim humour, someone had attached a 'Keep Music Live' decal to the casket. I was not ashamed to cry.

The Alex Welsh Band, in retrospect, reaped bleak harvests for lifetimes of devotion to Chicago jazz. Alex, Archie Semple, Fred Hunt, and Lennie Hastings all died early from the effects of alcohol. Written deep into the jazz contract of their times was the image of the hard-living, hard-drinking jazz man and they copied their idols. If Bix Beiderbecke and his legion followers had embraced death by sucking gumdrops then many artistic latercomers would have robbed the sweetshops at gunpoint in order to do exactly the same.

After Alex's death it was decided to take a 'Reunion' band on the road. Together, we broadcast for 'Jazz Club' and revisited several of Alex's old haunts, recreating the band's formula from poised ballad medleys to hilarious banjo and vocal features. The old magic felt as if it might be there forever and the Alex Welsh Legacy band still plays as a reminder of fine days gone by.

In 1983, while on tour around Lancashire with the Alex Welsh Reunion Band, I first met the entertainer Donald Swann who, with Michael Flanders, had created the immortal two-man review, 'At the Drop of a Hat', and its successors. A decade earlier, my father had introduced me to one of Donald's songs, 'Slow Train', and I'd fallen in love with it at first hearing.

We had just finished our lunchtime set at Nelson Jazz Club when a small birdlike man wearing circular horn-rimmed spectacles bustled in. I knew immediately that this was Donald, there to play a cabaret concert and we had an interesting conversation which I followed up with a letter suggesting a collaboration, possibly to be called 'Swann in Jazz'. Later we met to talk the idea over and Donald preceded subsequent meetings with tape after tape of original music and songs fusing classical, review and pop influences in a succession of what Lorenz Hart called 'constantly surprising refrains'.

'Dear Digby,' he said at one meeting, 'the idea of 'Swann in Jazz' delights me. *Delights me*, dear chap! But you must remember I'm a review performer. My songs rely on *rubato,* varying tempo in the music, dramatic pauses and such. I'm not sure it can survive on the straight ahead four to the bar swing of a jazz band.'

But I felt that the idea of setting Donald Swann's music in jazz surroundings might be worth pursuing, despite this technical conundrum. So, on trains and coach journeys across country, I listened and re-listened to tapes to identify songs of his that could live comfortably with a jazz treatment and gradually found some. They were beautiful songs too: some with religious themes, others distinctly secular, many hilarious and one or two with a contemporary pop slant in their makeup. Gradually, a show began to take shape but when we started to rehearse I realised how loudly an acoustic jazz band plays; Donald's voice was submerged under even the most gentle brush-stroke of Adrian Macintosh's cymbals. It was not at all a comfortable feeling but we pressed on, aware that we were in the presence of a premier British entertainer in the midst of some sort of re-awakening.

I visited Donald to discuss the show and was granted the privilege of an afternoon of quiet conversation in his garden. That day he talked widely about his life, his views on music and the world. A deeply committed Quaker, he had written a full catalogue of religious music and I asked him in passing if, as a Quaker, he celebrated Christmas.

'Well no, not really, Digby, dear fellow!' said Donald, in his wonderfully cultured Wodehousian manner. 'I suppose the implication of that would be that you are nicer to people at Christmas than at other times. We Quakers believe that you should try to be charitable all the year round!'

He had undertaken some extraordinary projects since Michael Flanders' death, among them setting to music the many songs of his old friend J.R. Tolkein's massive trilogy *Lord of the Rings* in the original Elvic. Donald was happy to talk about his legendary partnership with Michael Flanders and told me the story of how their collaboration had begun. At an undergraduate review rehearsal he had sung the light hearted but hoary couplet, 'My eyes are blind, I cannot see, I have not brought my specs with me!' Michael Flanders turned to his future partner and promptly sang back the couplet: 'He cannot see, his eyes are dim, he has not brought his specs with him!'

'There's a man with a genuine sense of humour,' thought Donald, and the pair of them were on their way.

Donald took infinite pains over our project, rehearsing, discussing, endlessly re-considering the finer points of his presentation's impact. Unlike my impatient self, he was also interested to hear everyone's views on how the show should develop and, bound for a daily lunch of egg and chips (at a cafe round the corner from his Battersea home), might well ask a newspaper vendor for musical advice if some doubt were on his mind.

'Swann in Jazz' made its debut at Sandra Schock's small theatre in Hassocks, Somerset. Sandra was a champion of Donald's music and had previously mounted a children's production of his show 'Lucy and the Hunter'. Several exquisite selections from 'Lucy' (among them a graceful lyrical song 'Cruel Is the Swallow') had been incorporated into our review. In the event it was well received. John Barnes, Bill Skeat, Ron Rubin, Len Skeat, Adrian Macintosh, Clive Pracey and Liza Lincoln all took part at various times and we went on to present 'Swann in Jazz' on the Isle of Man and for a short tour which even included one performance at Carnegie Hall – but in Dunfermline! It was just before this tour that I realised that Donald suffered more than his share of excruciating pre-performance agonies but, once on the stand, they seemed to disappear completely.

Right until his death from cancer a few years later, Donald spoke warmly of the possibility of a recording of 'Swann in Jazz' and subsequently Alison, his widow, pushed the project through by financing the issue of a CD of our very first concert for Sandra Schock in Sussex. It was a musically eccentric affair because, besides the natural problems of a first night performance, the show had been recorded direct to cassette on a four-track tape deck (one channel of which was dysfunctional). But with mixing, heavy editing, and the use of several studio tracks with dubbed applause, one of Donald Swann's last wishes was accomplished. I'm glad of that.

In 1983, the same year I met Donald, I was invited to take part in the M and B (Mitchells and Butler) Jam Session organised by Jim Simpson and held in Birmigham. This was a prestige concert in the Roman amphitheatre of Cannon Hill Park. The whole event was recorded live for Big Bear Records and led, one year later, to the formation of the Birmingham International Jazz Festival. Humphrey Lyttelton and I were the trumpeters there and around us was an all-star cast of British swing musicians including Bruce Turner.

For his 1984 M and B Jam session, Jim had decided to take full advantage of Bruce's presence. Thirty years before – just after Turner had joined Humphrey Lyttelton's band – fans at a Lyttelton concert at Birmingham Town Hall had raised a banner bearing the uncharitable message, *Go home, dirty bopper!* directed at the new arrival: a supposed bebop infiltrator, complete with saxophone, to the ranks of Lyttelton's once all-traditional band. So, Jim had a new banner made up! Long enough, at thirty feet, to carpet a corridor, it bore the same legend and was manfully shouldered by a small platoon of helpers. As Bruce launched into his opening solo, the unsteady crocodile rose to its feet and raised its banner. Halfway through, Turner opened his eyes momentarily to look out at the audience and accordingly corpsed for several bars before returning to his unflagging inspiration. The banner reappeared regularly throughout the evening accompanied by Bruce Turner's response of 'Dad! Dad! Great! Great!'

Once a year at the festival, Jim Simpson has dedicated a Guide Dog, naming it after an honoured visitor. Dogs delivered to grateful new owners down the years include 'Melly', 'Humph', and, one year, 'Digby' too.

'Would you mind a photocall?' Jim asked. 'At nine-thirty on the steps of the Town Hall.'

Of course not! So at nine-thirty I arrived, with several reporters and photographers, two or three attractive models from a local agency and my new friend Digby, an adorable floppy young Labrador in the first stage past puppydom, who nestled supportively between my knees on cue. Our photographer, looking as if he might have just got back from a night-long party, took his position on the steps and aimed a camera while I gently massaged behind Digby's ears. There was a short pause, during which at least one of the gorgeous models dissolved into laughter. I continued massaging, unaware that Digby had launched an erection that you could have seen from Coventry.

'Oh come on!' said my photographer irritably. 'We can't have that!'

But there didn't seem to be anything we could do. Flag tongued and genial, Digby was irrepressibly proud and his newly-acquired canine manhood continued to stand the test of time.

'Well, really,' insisted the photographer, looking more tired than ever, 'if we can't get him to put his thing away, we'll have to call it a day.'

Which, at least for a while, is what we had to do. Finally, photographs of Digby at rest were somehow produced and off he went, no doubt to a delighted new owner. My namesake is retired now but in the intervening years I imagined him skating across main roads and through traffic, helpless charge in tow, every time he caught sight of an attractive friend.

One example of Jim Simpson's generosity towards those he believes in musically involves a sad story of a great American trumpeter. Don Goldie's name is known still to jazz afficionados but his proven abilities on record – in Jack Teagarden's band amongst others – warrant a place amongst the greatest in the music's trumpet history.

Goldie was the last of the great dixieland trumpet stylists and his first recordings were in the impressive company of Buddy Rich. But everyone noticed him first with Teagarden's 1950s band. Teagarden called him, 'the greatest I've ever heard,' and this was praise indeed given that Jack was Louis Armstrong's lifelong friend. On records of the period, Goldie's exuberance explodes in glorious fireworks alongside his bemused trombonist-leader. Flyaway triple-tonguing, like a joyful circus trumpeter, decorates the music at appropriate moments and flowing trumpet rhapsodies, as open hearted as anything by Harry James, soar above the ensemble. And yet – within a couple of years of his recognition as a major talent – jazz succumbed to the music of the rock generations and Don Goldie was as good as forgotten, though occasionally rumours of him still spread around the scene.

'He's the trumpet king of Miami, Florida these days,' my friend Keith Ingham told me during the 1980s, 'and he has a music agency. Puts out bands around the area.'

But then, one day in 1988, on the answerphone there was a message. 'Hi! I don't know if anyone there knows my name – but this is Don Goldie. I'm trying to contact someone called Digby Fairweather ... I'd really like to hear from you!'

I was back on the phone in an instant. 'Is this really Don Goldie? I don't believe it!'

The conversation that followed was a long one. I talked about how his music had rung through my house and my youth and how his trumpet playing continued to inspire me. 'Are you playing as much as ever?' I asked. There was a pause.

'Well,' said Goldie, 'there isn't quite as much work as there was. And playing around the house can be depressing. But I work very hard to keep my chops in shape, Digby – as I'm sure you do! Every day I make myself play a forty-minute set, non-stop, here in my house. And you know something? Around Miami they call me 'Little Al' because I sub for Al Hirt!' Hirt was a trumpet phenomenon – as well as a household name – in America for over thirty years.

'Sometimes,' said Don, 'I call people up under an assumed identity. It's easier that way, you know? And I can negotiate a little more toughly for my services!'

'You should be working all of the time, Don,' I said, meaning it, 'Much more than some of those newer players around.'

I named a name. Goldie agreed and it was apparent that my new acquaintance, like many of the greatest of his craft, possessed the necessary ten percent of steel under his affable exterior. I asked him about his own favourite trumpeters.

'Well, Pops, of course,' said Don. 'But, after that, Billy Butterfield. I copied everything from Billy.' His voice, as it regularly did, warmed over into pure sentiment.

'But you did so much that Billy never thought of. How about those wonderful octave-leaps you played so perfectly on the records. They're impossible!'

'Oh no. They all came from Billy really, you know! By the way, you're living with your mother just now? That's great. I loved my mother very much. But I lost her just a while ago.' For a moment his voice dropped, and he sounded lost.

This was to be the first of many conversations. Long-playing records, letters, souvenirs, even tee-shirts arrived from Florida. It seemed criminal that no-one would bring Don Goldie to Britain. But after several years, my friend Jim Simpson took the chance and came up with an offer.

'We'll bring him to Ronnie Scott's at Birmingham for a week,' promised Jim. 'And we'll pay the air fare – plus a reasonable fee.' When that offer materialised, I allowed myself the rare privilege of an evening off to drink a bottle of whisky, and play my well-worn copy of 'Think Well of Me', with its celebration of the music of Willard Robison by Don Goldie and Jack Teagarden. Then, rather too drunk for comfort, I rolled up the stairs to my office, just to ring Don and tell him the news and how much I loved his music, and him.

A tiny voice, quite unlike Don (or his phantom agent) spoke the hollow word 'Hello', and I felt the phone freeze in my grasp. 'No,' I thought, 'this is silly. You're drunk and he's not. This is eveningtime, and there it's two o'clock in the afternoon. And this is not your closest buddy. Put the phone down!' Click.

A day later I wrote to Don with the offer of Jim's trip to England and posted it off, airmail special. Two nights later, there was a message on my answerphone, 'Dig, this is Jim Simpson. John Chilton tells me that Don Goldie is dead. Have you heard anything? Let me know.'

It was true. Don Goldie – the high-flying trumpet man – had gone to hospital and discovered a daunting illness. So, he discharged himself, wrote out a list of the people he would prefer not to attend the funeral to come, and blew his brains out with a shotgun.

In 1985, I noticed that TV producer Laurence Vulliamy had recently recorded a show celebrating 'Forty years of Humphrey Lyttelton' and dropped him a line suggesting that 'Fifty years of Nat Gonella' might be an even more spectacular idea. He agreed, and the show (for Channel Four) was scheduled for a live concert in the appropriate surroundings of Southsea Pier. Accordingly, all my friends from our 1983 'We Remember Nat' tour arrived on set at ten in the morning. The star, however, seemed as if he might not appear at all. 'I'm usually having a bet at this time of day,' he said on the morning of the recording. Laurence sent a limousine.

But when he did arrive, everything went wonderfully. Ex-Georgians Pat Smuts and Tiny Winters were interviewed by compère Benny Green, Humphrey Lyttelton (in a tiger suit) joined us for a finale on 'Tiger Rag' and Nat sang many of his hits with our six-piece band. Included was a nicely-chaotic version of 'I Must See Annie Tonight' – a lyrically complicated song he recorded originally in America in 1939 with Benny Carter, Buster Bailey and friends.

We later recorded an album for the American label Jazzology, based on the music from our show, with the full cast plus Dave Lee on piano and Liza Lincoln. The tracks we recorded included four backings over which Nat had agreed to overdub vocals, including what I thought was a ravishing – and potentially highly emotional – version of 'September Song'. The sentiments of this popular masterpiece seemed to fit Nat – and his last wife Dorothy – to perfection. After the tapes were recorded I sent a cassette down to Gosport for Nat's approval, and was mystified when, a couple of weeks later, Liza delivered some bad news.

'Nat's rung,' she said, 'and he doesn't want to do the record.'

'Why?' I asked, dismayed.

'Well, he says he just doesn't want to do any more.'

This was a disappointment of course, but stupidly I decided to abandon the project for the moment, rather than to ask Nat why he'd changed his mind. Although the decision seemed unreasonable, he was retired (and entitled to make decisions about his own activities) and the last thing I wanted to do was to upset my friend. So, we found a spectacular deputy, Wild Bill Davison. I'd always enjoyed the Wild One's singing and we made the journey to promoter Dave Bennett's studio to dub on the missing vocals. Wild Bill's chosen position to record was with Liza sitting on his knee and his version of 'September Song' was as poignant as any I can remember.

But despite our eminent guest, I couldn't help feeling that the idea had lost its central focus and for several years put the project to one side. Producer George Buck – a munificent benefactor to jazz and regularly dubbed 'Saint George' by people in the know – forbore either to enquire what had happened to his record, or to ask for his money back. It wasn't until 1996 that Liza persuaded me that the music might still be worth releasing. After re-listening, I knew that she was right and soon afterwards solved the mystery of why Nat had turned down the project so unexpectedly. We would have recorded his vocals in a recording studio, of course, but Nat had mistakenly thought that he somehow had to record his vocals onto the cassette I had sent him. He valiantly spent several hours wrestling at home with a borrowed karaoke machine in an attempt to record *al fresco* before deciding that this really was all too much trouble. Our album came out in any case and to my delight won 'Record of the Month' award in Jazzology's radio show, hosted by George Buck in New Orleans.

As the 1980s progressed, my visits to Stan Barker in Clitheroe became more frequent and were a blessed change of pace from a professional scene that was plainly – in writer-photographer Val Wilmer's words – 'as serious as your life'. With him it was possible to relax, to assume a more comfortable pace, and steadily to pursue our developing preoccupation, jazz in education.

At first Stan wrote down the musical exercises we brought to our classes, but later the two of us tended to work by ear. In between those two processes, over five years or so, we learned a great deal quickly. We first had to specify what we were doing when we improvised and then learn how to explain the process clearly and correctly to beginners. Furthermore Stan and I were both mainstream players and setting out the principles behind the playing of latterday musicians from John Coltrane to Ornette Coleman was initially a challenge. A young guitarist came to us calmly at the end of a Jazz College weekend course to have a quiet word. 'I just thought I should tell you,' he said, with no show of anger, 'that I haven't got what I needed from this.'

It seemed to me, from that moment, inescapable that we would have to arm ourselves with state of the art knowledge of improvisational theory. So, in the early 1980s, I walked the length of Charing Cross Road to buy every book on theories of jazz education that looked worth examining. Then came six weeks of concentrated effort in which we gave ourselves a crash course in contemporary jazz instruction. At the end of it, Jazz College emerged with a good deal of renewed confidence.

As work gathered speed, it seemed there was no stopping us. We established strong educational links with Northern Ireland and Belfast Youth Jazz Orchestra and these Irish links prompted an invitation to teach together for Arthur Aitchison and Belfast Music School. Stan encountered a fire on the ferry bringing him to Ireland; then we met and, by dramatic mischance, arrived in Belfast city centre at the exact moment of IRA hunger striker Bobby Sands' tragic death. Armed troops were on the streets and it seemed as if a storm of violence was about to burst. No taxis were running, and Stan found a phone booth, only to discover that he phone had been angrily torn from its connections. From the box he disappeared into a bar to use the public phone and, soon after, a cab arrived.

'You didn't phone from the bar back there?' queried the driver.

'Yes,' said Stan, whose ashen face by this time matched mine. 'Why not?'

'That's an IRA headquarters,' returned the driver. 'If they'd known who you were they'd have sent one of their cabs and you'd have ended up down an alley!'

'Is there a bar at the hotel?' Stan inquired weakly.

We returned to Belfast a number of times and also continued teaching at Southport Arts Centre where, one year later, we recorded 'Let's Duet', an album that subsequently achieved a high poll position in America's *Cadence* magazine. My playing was at its peak and Stan, as ever, was the perfect musical partner for cornet-piano duets.

Our Tuesday night duet sessions in Southport's 'T'other bar', underpinned by Stan's two-handed piano, were becoming well-known all over the area too. Week by week, music-teachers, musicians, pupils and friends gathered to listen to what, for me, was the best music-making up to now in my playing career. In 1986, two marvellous friends, Steve and Jenny Voce came across and recorded us live for BBC Radio Merseyside. Steve gave the tapes to Jazz College and these sessions, with our original 'Let's Duet' LP, make up the 'Something to Remember Us By' double CD later issued by George Buck on his Jazzology label: probably my own favourite on-record music so far.

As Stan was the principal organiser, Jazz College's activities almost always ran smoothly. One day, however, I had been asked if we would play a concert at Bury St. Edmunds near Colchester in Essex and told Stan. Unfortunately I used the abbreviation 'Bury' – a small town, no more than an hour from Stan's home – and as the afternoon wore on and Stan and I chatted together, I began to detect an unexpected relaxation in my friend's view of the journey.

'Stanley,' I queried at last, 'shouldn't we be on our way?'

'No, old friend,' came the response. 'Bury's only an hour away.'

'Oh hell!' I said, falling in at last. 'The place is Bury St. Edmunds.'

We made Bury St. Edmunds with ten minutes to go, though Stan's conversation was marginally more clipped than usual as we accelerated down the motorway.

On another occasion, while working in a school with Stan, I noticed a sad long-faced boy with a cornet hovering near to our group and invited him to sit by me in the class. I'll refer to this boy as Harry and his class teacher told me, 'He's a good boy but he's had a lot of troubles, and is probably going to be transferred to a special needs school quite soon.' Week by week, Harry sat near to me, playing the cornet but seldom saying anything. Then one day he approached me and spoke – still a rare occurrence. 'I'm going to come across to Southport to see you for lessons at the Arts Centre,' he volunteered.

As the months drew on, I slowly got to know my young friend. His father, whom he adored, had left when Harry was in his early teens, and his mother had found it difficult to fill the gap. Rapidly he had withdrawn from life, turning inwards to misery. Perhaps jazz music might provide the beginnings of a route out again. Gradually Harry's playing improved and one day, surveying his short-model cornet, he decided that it was time to look for a proper trumpet. So together we made the trip across from Southport to Rushworth's Music Store in Liverpool (the legendary shop which supplied the Beatles with their guitars early on) and found a new instrument. Harry joined our evening classes at Southport, became a regular visitor to our Tuesday duo sessions and gradually began to talk more easily and to smile. After a while there was no more talk of a 'special school'. We became true friends and Harry became like a son to me. Gentle and receptive, he had changed completely from the withdrawn unhappy boy I had met a year or two earlier. Today he is a professional trumpet player and I'm proud of him.

As knowledge of our work with Jazz College spread we were asked to work further afield and gradually made our way along the coast from Southport into Liverpool. Some of the schools were superb: Maricourt, with its music course run by a gifted teacher and jazz singer, Jackie Colhoun, was a constant joy to visit. But others were harder going and on one occasion we were detailed to visit a very tough school indeed, in the area of Liverpool that broadcaster Peter Clayton once called 'Brutal Bootle'. The music master, Sid Foot, a rudimentary trombonist, liked the idea of jazz musicians in school, an enthusiasm not altogether shared by his headmaster, who met us in the school foyer.

'This'll bring you down from your ivory towers,' he warned us.

And he was right. As we made our tentative way into the school music room, an unidentified flying object flew past my head. It turned out to be a euphonium. Eight or ten pupils were busy playing football with instruments, banging them on desks or dismembering them just for fun. One of the biggest boys pushed his face into Stan's.

'Ere,' he yelled, 'are you called Barker 'cos you're a dog?'

'Ha ha!' said Stanley compliantly. The inquisitor warmed to his job.

'And is this bloke called Digby 'cos he's a pig?' Another euphonium flew past. Stan smiled weakly and embarked on our standard routine of musical exercises in spite of the happy oblivion which greeted them.

Such schools were horrifying prospects but teaching a responsive, talented class how to improvise was, by contrast, a source of deep pleasure and fulfilment. Every commitment was different: a carefully conceived teaching plan might succeed admirably in one classroom and fail next day in another. Thinking on our feet, judging a class, knowing when to turn on the heat or relax – all these challenges were very much like playing jazz: you can never be sure whether success or failure will follow on. All you can do is prepare – then pray.

In 1986, Chris Clarke was appointed as curator of the National Sound Archive Jazz Division, a branch of the British Library that aimed to collect every jazz record from cylinder to CD. This was an exciting new development: a national organisation as well-respected as the British Library was embracing jazz as a serious musical art-form.

Chris, a part-time saxophonist, had begun – amongst a number of other good projects – the 'British Oral Jazz History', a comprehensive set of one-to-one interviews with important British jazz musicians from George Chisholm to Evan Parker which could run into several recording hours and, as a wise policy, were conducted by fellow musicians. It wasn't long before Chris asked me to conduct several such interviews and in ensuing months we talked to Fred Hunt (not long before his death), George Chisholm, Jimmy Skidmore, Tommy McQuater, Tiny Winters and Harry Gold.

Harry is one of Britain's most remarkable musicians and British jazz's longest survivor. Until the age of ninety-four, he was playing bass-saxophone with undiminished vigour and skill and leading his legendary Pieces of Eight, which began in

1940 as a band-within-a-band for Oscar Rabin. His continuing health he attributed to two sources: a steady morning workout (involving twenty press-ups) and thereafter an equally steady intake of Irish Whiskey.

Harry was born in Ireland but moved to England in the first week of his life. He is nevertheless proud of his birthright still and relapses regularly into a broad Irish brogue after a drink or two. And this happened on the day that Chris and I interviewed him at his Holborn home for the National Sound Archive. It was a long and fascinating story which, at lunchtime, Harry brought to a temporary close with the words, 'so in 1926 I joined the Metronomes at the Astoria, Charing Cross Road!' Chris and I turned off our recorder and all three of us went to a nearby pub to enjoy lunch. Harry, in turn, enjoyed several large glasses of Jameson's Irish whiskey chased with Guinness and rapidly turned into a loquacious Irishman! By the time we got back to the recorder at two o'clock his voice had altered completely from the Englishman who had finished talking at mid-day. As Chris turned on his recorder again I asked, 'So how about the Metronomes?'

'Well, sure enough,' said dear Harry, in leprechaun mode. 'T'was the neatest little band you ever heard, no doubt of that!' And on he went, in 'Finian's Rainbow' style. Future generations of researchers may wonder why – within the space of a sentence – a completely different voice takes up Harry Gold's story midway through his British Oral Jazz History interview but that's the reason.

Like Kenny Baker, Harry Hayes, Nat Gonella and others, Harry is superbly untouched by time and somewhere in his mid-80s asked John Barnes, a proud member and regular visitor to Lords' Cricket Ground, if he could possibly join the MCC. John was delighted with the request. 'But Harry,' he said, 'the waiting list is something like ten years!'

'I don't mind waiting,' declared Harry, unperturbed.

All through his life Harry has supported Musicians' Union activities and the jazz accordionist Tony Compton remembers an example of this. 'One night,' he told me, 'Harry's

Pieces of Eight came to Southend and us young lads were playing support for him. Just before we went on stage, in came the organiser. "Are you boys in the Union? Because if you're not you'd better fill in these forms right now – or Harry Gold's not going on." So – we had to join, there and then!'

Digby and Stan Barker as Humph saw us!

7.

trumpet blues or trouble on the high Cs.

In the mid-1980s, writing and playing were, luckily, keeping me very busy. I had bought a tiny flat back in Southend and felt deep relief at leaving London for the familiar streets of my hometown. After all, I'd run a career reasonably success-fully from Southend up until the mid-1970s – so why carry on trying to be a Londoner? No reason.

I was getting used to the life of a professional jazzman and was playing more strongly than I had for years, technique fully restored, and with a style that was starting to owe a lot to Warren Vaché Jnr. By practising exercises recommended by Tommy McQuater and Ruby Braff, I had acquired immense stylistic fluidity. Performance was now a carefree thing, studios no longer held fears and recording sessions were events to look forward to. For now, everything was fine and dandy.

By 1986 my playing had reached a peak. I was playing concerts with Stan Barker, and with bands around the country, and life had never felt easier. Recording sessions and broadcasts were effortless and even in the dull dry acoustics of a studio my cornet sang. Like Warren Vaché, I'd perfected the technique of playing up in the instrument's altissimo register with the soft singing ease of a violin, a gift that I had acquired at the (possibly dangerous) cost of adjusting my embouchure.

Amongst many other jobs at that period, I was working and broadcasting with Brian Priestley's Special Septet, a prestigious group including Olaf Vas, Derek Wadsworth and my old friend Don Rendell. Trombonist Tony Milliner also asked me to join his group, Mingus Revisited. This was a challenge and I enjoyed exploring the Mingus arrangements that Tony had transcribed from records, note for note. They were often fascinatingly voiced but also occasionally incomprehensible: doubled fifths for two saxophones in a four-piece front line, producing an effect that was either definitively original or simply a hasty mistake. Either way, it was Mingus.

In 1987, another pleasure was to welcome a real legend – trombonist Spiegle 'The Beagle' Willcox – to London. Spiegle, in his late eighties, was the last surviving member of Jean Goldkette's Orchestra where he had played with Bix Beiderbecke. Later, when most of Goldkette's sidemen moved on to Paul Whiteman's orchestra, he had given up full-time music to make a successful living in his family's mining business. So successful indeed that, by the time I met this big, gentle old musician with his mischievous twinkle and rumbustious trombone style, he had a prestigious single line address. 'Cincinnatus, New York' was all you needed to reach him by mail.

Despite his wealth, Spiegle Willcox was a shy man with a ready laugh who travelled regularly with his daughter to jazz commitments around the world. His return to playing had been prompted by Joe Venuti, who had encouraged his old colleague to play a few clubs and festivals. Once his trombone playing was back on form, Spiegle began to work on his own, and in London together we played a 'Tribute to Bix' concert for promoter Michael Webber at the South Bank's Queen Elizabeth Hall. A couple of days later, this grand old man joined us on a Riverboat shuffle for fun. Sitting near the band at one point, he began reminiscing about Bix Beiderbecke and, aware that every word was gold, I committed the cardinal sin of asking him to wait a second, then reached for a tape-recorder and turned it on. Spiegle did what every interviewee does in such circumstances: he started thinking about his thoughts and dried up.

However, as a close friend of Joe Venuti, he was a fresh fund of stories about the premier swing violinist and arch practical joker. One concerned Wingy Manone, the one-armed trumpeter to whom Venuti once sent one cuff-link as a Christmas present. Spiegle told it this way. Wingy had just learned to drive and one day Venuti rang up to ask if he wanted to do a week's work at a club out of town.

'Sure,' said Wingy, 'I can drive now!'

'Well,' said Joe, 'it's a long way. Take down these instructions, Wingston. Drive out of New York on Highway 6 then drive around three hundred miles and on to Highway 51. Two hours along there and then take 98 for another coupla hundred miles, and then you'll find yourself getting near. The Club's on the outskirts on Beech Street which you'll hit as you come off the highway. It's called the Figaro. Be there for seven.'

Wingy agreed and early in the morning began his long drive, gradually leaving the New York skyline behind and heading for wide open spaces. All day he drove with Venuti's instructions on the dashboard until nine hours later he was disturbed to see the New York skyline re-appear. The club was four blocks from his apartment!

Before I saw Spiegle for the last time another hilarious situation arose. We were due to play the Soho Jazz Festival and to be joined by the legendary bebop altoist Frank Morgan. For players like Morgan, bebop is more than a category, it's a proud banner. To play with him, I had assembled a trio – Brian Lemon, Dave Green and drummer Andy Trim – that knew the style inside out and we were all set to go.

On the first set at Dean Street, however, I was delighted to see Spiegle walk into the club. Would he come and join us for a tune or two? Certainly! So, underpinned by Brian Lemon's striding, Jess Stacy-esque piano and Dave Green's firm two-

Brian Lemon

in-the-bar bass we launched into a spirited dixieland hack through 'Hard Hearted Hannah'. Right in the middle, modern jazzman Frank Morgan walked in and stood transfixed. I went across to introduce myself and explain.

'I can't play with you guys,' he said, brushing aside my greeting. 'I'm a bebop alto player!' In the club, in the midst of a number, it was hard to explain that Brian and Dave played with Peter King or Milt Jackson as easily and with as much enjoyment as they played dixieland, and that at the drop of a glove they could switch to Frank Morgan's stylistic needs. But he was up the steps and out of the club before Hannah had finished pouring water on her drowning man.

During the two years from 1985, I had been busy with my co-authors, Ian Carr and Brian Priestley, assembling *Jazz: The Essential Companion* and begun to take my new and fluid ease of technique for granted. I was beginning to build a discography of value and became indolent as playing seemed easy. Then I stopped practising. But as the summer weeks of 1987 went by, I found myself pressing my trumpet mouthpiece ever-harder into my top-lip for those seductive viola-soft altissimo notes and noticing that something seemed to be slightly amiss. While playing high on my cornet was still easy,

I seemed to be working harder to produce the notes lower down – an inexplicable reversal of the standard experience of playing any brass instrument.

Then, one evening in 1987, while playing duos with Stan Barker on our regular Tuesday night down in T'other Bar at Southport Arts Centre, it happened. Shifting my embouchure to aim for one of my peach-gentle high notes, a tearing pain sliced down the side of my right cheek and down to my neck and chest. I was shaken and stopped playing. Was this a stroke?

It wasn't, but for the next month unaccountable and terrifying things began to happen. All the bottom notes on my cornet became impossible to produce. A frightening twitch as I headed for once-easy notes distorted one side of my face. Sympathy pains ran from the top of my head to the base of my neck and down the side of my chest. And, as I helplessly continued to try and perform over the next week or two, my entire cornet technique toppled, then collapsed completely. Every atom of control over the instrument I had learned to play so easily waved goodbye, then vanished.

To begin with, the horrifying scope of the tragedy seemed insurmountable. What had happened? I simply didn't know. 'That looks bad,' said a brass advisor and brass band soloist, Fred Shaw, in north London. 'You need six months off, at least.' Good advice, but how to pay the rent, meantime?

There are cures for a tired lip but this was more than fatigue: it seemed very much like permanent damage. I told my friend, the critic Clarrie Henley, who had watched with delight my retransformation into a superbly confident player over the last five years, 'Oh no, Dig,' he said chillingly, 'not again.' In my early professional years, pressure had taken the shine from my playing once already. Now I had clambered back into the public eye and ear, only to suffer a further collapse.

This was a bitter, bitter time. In a flash, I could no longer broadcast or record with the ease of the last four years. Recording sessions became an object of terror, outside broadcasts a matter for hastily erected alibis which put me at log-gerheads with one unsympathetic BBC producer for a couple of years after. At home I struggled day in, day out, with a problem for which no-one could supply an answer. As Noel Coward once said, 'I know nothing so dreary as the feeling that you can't make the sounds or write the words that your whole creative being is yearning for.'

At my invitation, several people tried to help. Tenorist Bill Skeat advised by phone and BBC Big Band trumpeter Paul Eshelby took a look at my unlovely problem and twitching face as I tried to blow. One horrific south London teacher decided the problem must be psychological and fashioned a sort of home-made therapy. 'Blow harder,' instructed my guru. 'Now scream!' It didn't work. Nor did it work when I enlisted with a local physiotherapist who took on the problem as a challenge, prescribing daily facial exercises and strapping small terminals to my embouchure for electronic injections. But I knew as well as my helpers that they had no idea how to sort out such a problem and that I was getting nowhere. To be able to do something very well is a gift. To have that gift rudely and suddenly snatched away is a double bitterness because you know of the capabilities within you.

To stop playing completely was out of the question. So, the first thing was to somehow create the illusion that I could still lead a band – and play the trumpet just as well. Accordingly, I wrote a complete library for my band of friends, the Superkings, which confined my trumpet parts to the (very) few notes I could still play. My colleagues accepted the situation with bemused tolerance and Dave Shepherd did his best, with the rest, to joke me through what was an appallingly difficult time. Roy Williams tried to help too. 'What's up, mate?' he asked one morning at coffee, very soon after a night at the Jersey Jazz Festival where my efforts were making for painful listening. Vainly, as he listened patiently, I tried to explain that I didn't know what had happened either.

In a very short time my appalling level of performance was recognised by quite a lot of the jazz community, despite the fact that I had determined – for self-preservation's sake – to keep the news low-profile. In Jersey, I joined a hotel foyer jam session with fellow guests, watching them drift away hastily after one crippled number was completed.

But somehow I continued to work. And, of course, there were lighter moments too. One occurred when I appeared with the Superkings on the late Sir Harry Secombe's long-running Sunday programme, 'Highway'. To record this series, Sir Harry took to the road in a gigantic mobile home which, for our show, had set down at my beloved childhood haunt, Flatford Mill, deep in Constable country in Suffolk. We were to record an interview at the millside and I was thrilled at the thought of meeting a lifelong hero. As jolly as you'd expect, regularly inserting fruity raspberries into the midst of semi-serious conversation, Sir Harry had no objection to recalling the glory days of the Goons. 'Eccles, you know,' he reminded me, 'could be quite profound. Remember that wonderful one-liner when Neddy asks him "What are you doing in that coal cellar?" and Eccles says, "Everybody's got to be somewhere!" Perfect!'

Prior to our film-shoot for 'Highway', the Superkings and I had recorded our item – my reworking of 'Song of Songs' – at Wembley's magnificent CTS Studios. A week or so later we travelled to Flatford to mime to our track for film purposes in the library of Willie Lott's Cottage on the banks of the river. That evening, the producer, Hugh de las Casas, tele-phoned. 'I'm sorry,' he said, 'there's a problem.'

'Oh dear,' I said, 'I do hope it wasn't us.'

'No,' said Hugh. 'On the contrary. It's us! We shot you in black and white by mistake. You're going to have to come down again.'

'Does that mean,' I asked cautiously, 'that we get paid again?'

'Oh yes,' said Hugh, audibly biting his lip.

So down we went again and re-shot the sequence, this time in colour.

Years later, Jack Parnell, who conducted the ATV Orchestra

over many years, told me of an event in which Sir Harry had a part. On one show at the London Palladium a visiting star had dropped out and it was decided to ask the incomparable singer Placido Domingo to step in. 'He'd decided to do 'O Sole Mio',' explained Jack, 'but hadn't got an arrangement. So we asked the librarian and she found the one that Harry Secombe used. So we got to the rehearsal fast and Placido was in full flight when I turned over the score – and the music suddenly turned into 'Yes We Have No Bananas'!'

Although I was still working with the Superkings, my playing had gone right back to the start. What else could I do if playing should one day prove impossible? I could always carry on with writing commissions, I supposed: *Grove's Dictionary of Jazz* for one thing – an exciting new publishing project for which, over the months to come, I became a senior contributor.

So, frustrated that I was barely able to touch the trumpet, I applied myself to other issues, including campaigning about the predicament that Stan Barker and I had talked of so much across the years: the invidious life conditions of the jazz performer. Over the two years from 1987 to 1989, I set up and attended the meetings and wrote the reports that established the Association of British Jazz Musicians. The ABJM – first espoused then faithfully administered by my old friend Chris Hodgkins, the newly-appointed director of Jazz Services – was set up in 1987 as the first professional association for jazz musicians in Britain. But it has taken time to achieve any sort of wide recognition and by 1990 membership was temporarily falling. It was at this point that Maurice Jennings, General Secretary of the Musicians' Union, wrote a letter to Chris. 'It's a shame that things aren't working,' Maurice said, 'but jazz musicians will always resist corporate attempts at help, or even organisation; they're rogue elephants and nothing can be done!'

Seldom have I been so incensed by a written statement. Maurice, a good and decent man, was a well-liked friend to many in the jazz profession. His elegant tenor playing had been regularly heard when he was an invited sitter-in with Alex Welsh's great band back in the 1960s. Nevertheless, I wrote down my views in a report called *Jazz and the Musicians' Union* which included a list of positive proposals for the future, amongst them a revolutionary idea: the setting up of a jazz section within the Union. This report was submitted to Union headquarters and ruffled a few feathers in the process. But delegates, including Brian Blain and (admirably) Maurice Jennings, came to the ABJM with a proposal. 'First, Maurice answers Digby's report in print,' said Brian. 'Then you, Digby, redraft your report, without all those references to Maurice. Then we'll talk!'

Maurice's official rebuke and rebuttal arrived and, to save raised blood pressure, I threw it into the dustbin without reading a word. So that when likeable Maurice met me at the next ABJM meeting, and jokingly went 'on guard' like a boxer preparing for a flurry of blows, I was able to smile brightly and shake him warmly by the hand.

It was agreed that at a forthcoming Musicians' Union Annual Conference I might present a formal submission for the establishment of a jazz section. There was no guarantee that I'd be successful. After all, my colleagues argued, there was (at the time) no country and western section – and none for pop music either, come to that. Specialist musical groups were discouraged within the Musicians' Union, by and large. And yet I knew there should be a jazz section because this great art form has unique problems to which there are solutions. So, in 1992, I presented my paper at Winchester to the Annual Conference. Conference colleagues heard my address, the vote was taken and by an overwhelming majority it was agreed there should be a jazz section. It came into being the following year.

And so, soon after, did an old people's home for jazz musicians, The Good Companions, master-minded and financed by David and Jennifer Moffatt – two dear friends – in Churchtown, Southport. It is modelled on the showbusiness

140   *notes from a jazz life*

retirement home, Brinkworth House in Twickenham, and is the first of its kind for jazz musicians in Britain.

In these dark times, there was something else to work for. A National Jazz Archive had been a dream since 1985 when I first met Chris Clark, curator of the National Sound Archive Jazz Division. It occurred to me immediately that no such parallel archive facility existed for books about jazz (or, come to that, magazines, memorabilia, posters or photographs) but after a meeting with Chris and senior British Library executives it was obvious that they had neither time, space nor inclination to cover this related area. So after some thought I went to see my old friend and former employer, Frank Easton, by now deputy county librarian of Essex.

'Well,' said Frank, after a pause, 'there's a small office in the corner of the Reference Division of Loughton Central Library over at Traps Hill, near Epping. We might be able to let you have that for a while.'

With the help of Rob Froud and Elaine Adams (senior staff at Loughton), I sorted into order our first-ever donation, a random collection of books which the collector Chips Chipperfield had left to his friend, the late drummer Brian Chadwick, to be bequeathed to such an archive (should it ever exist).

These much prized first acquisitions – everything from books to tiny newspaper-cuttings which Chips had carried affectionately about in his wallet – were speedily augmented by more, including donations from Graham Langley, the long-time director of his own innovative British Institute of Jazz Studies at Ascot which pre-dated our own archive by almost thirty years. Graham selflessly saw no threat from our project – which admittedly offered public access as opposed to his own private enquiry service – and amongst much invaluable material gave us the *Melody Maker* 1942-84, an irreplaceable resource. In turn, I wrote off to firms of library binders including Remploy and Dunn and Wilson who agreed to bind our new acquisitions free of charge! I had offered these generous firms a free concert in return for their help but (no doubt fortunately at this playing point in my career) neither organisation got around to accepting the offer.

Then, one Saturday, the telephone rang and, 'Hello,' said a voice, 'I've heard about your Archive, and wonder, do you have the *Melody Maker*? Because I have some.'

'Well, thank you, but we do have the *Melody Maker* from 1942-84 – a very long run already.'

'Well, that's fine! Because I have 1926 – the year the paper started – to 1942! Shall I bring them round now?' At this point I was sure that God was on our side.

The Archive was launched by Charles Fox in 1989 at a merry gathering including dozens of jazz musicians and fans. Charles looked cautiously at our collection, which at that point was probably smaller than his own, subsequently left to us in his will. But things grew rapidly and, after its re-location to a big, new sunny room, the Archive was triumphantly re-launched by John Dankworth and Dame Cleo Laine who cut the ribbon in 1992. I took special pleasure in watching senior members of the profession including John, Cleo, Dave Shepherd and Benny Green, looking back at the heritage of their press cuttings over forty years or more. Everyone was happy, it seemed, except for Benny who momentarily looked sad. I asked him why.

'I wish,' said Benny reflectively, 'that I'd allowed myself to enjoy it more.'

In our new room, from the windows of which you can see the deep-green rim of Epping Forest, we were able to extend our activities and editions of Richard Willcox's long-running Radio 2 panel show 'Jazz Score' were recorded there. Over the next few years, archivists were appointed (first Ken Jones and then David Nathan). Open days, concerts and 'celebrity lectures' all became possible and in 1998 our trio of lecturers comprised pianist/composer Stan Tracey, bass player Jack Fallon and the great drummer/composer Tony Crombie. Together they formed a panel to discuss the founding days of British bebop but predictably the terms of reference widened out to allow some hilarious tales. One involved Alan Clare and this is exactly how Tony Crombie told the story.

'At one club in London,' he recalled, 'they'd given Alan a piano with a mirror panel so that he could see who was behind him. One night, just as he was in the middle of an exquisite and thoughtful version of Duke Ellington's 'In a Sentimental Mood', an enormous Scotsman, complete with kilt and dagger, loomed up and demanded, "D'ye know 'Annie Laurie'?" Then, without even a key for reference, he sang the whole thing triple-forte before making his departure.

'Alan was staggered and ten minutes later was telling me the story, still at the piano stool. "All of a sudden this bloody great Scotsman comes out of nowhere and right in the middle of my ballad barges in and yells at me 'D'you know 'Annie Laurie'?' and then sings the whole sodding thing straight through ..." At which point Alan glances in the piano-mirror and spots the Scotsman standing directly behind him. "And do you know ...?" Alan finished hastily, "it was one of the best things I've ever heard!"'

Stan Tracey – normally reluctant to waste too many words on the business of playing music – similarly came up with a beauty, just after we'd called time. 'I was playing with Trevor Watts, John Stevens – a whole team from the Spontaneous Music Ensemble,' Stan remembered, 'and everyone was blowing completely free – as loud as they could! So very softly, underneath, I played 'God Save the Queen' in block-chords – and nobody even noticed.'

This irreverent tale should not obscure the fact that Stan is a magnificent free musician and that his well-remembered duets with altoist Mike Osborne remain some of the greatest music ever recorded in that genre.

One day, during those years when the Archive was just getting started, I was reading down the 'For Sale' column in the back of *Jazz Journal International* and noticed the remarkable entry 'Louis Armstrong's trumpet for sale, £175'. Following a phone call to the number listed, I broke the land speed record from

Loughton – where I was spending a working day – to Kent to find out if this miracle could be true. At Sevenoaks I rushed out of the station, then – via a taxi – out of town to a line of old-style terraced cottages with, at their end, the address I had been given. My host's sitting room was full of cornet-cases, each of them containing a collector's gem, and when I had viewed his collection with considerable envy my new acquaintance lifted a long, cream-coloured case from a shelf. 'Here it is!' he said. And in the case, winking from the reflect-ed lights of the room, I saw a mint-condition 'Louis Armstrong Special' trumpet in bright superbly-engraved silver.

'There you are!' said my host. 'It's the one Louis designed with Henri Selmer in Paris around 1932. You see it in all his pictures. I picked up this one in Charing Cross Road, back in 1948.'

'It's beautiful,' I gasped, holding the superbly balanced instrument in my left hand and making as if to blow a note.

'Yes, it is,' said the owner. I took a deep breath.

'But you know – the fact is this instrument is worth *far* more than you're asking. To a collector – it's priceless.'

He looked at me steadily. 'Yes. But do you *like* it?'

'Like it? I love it! I'd mortgage my house!'

'Then write me a cheque. And take it. It's yours!'

I wrote the cheque and took this wonderful instrument home with me.

It was at this time, while living with Ena in Canewdon, that I contracted a serious bout of bronchitis. Pneumonia was on the cards and for several days I took steroids to cure a painful chest. While I was getting over this setback a copy of *Exchange and Mart* proved its worth with two telephone numbers. The first of them I'd looked up after the rigours of lying alone in bed for several days had begun to plant a strain in the normal male area. 'Phone Raunchy Rita,' said the advertisement, 'for an intimate chat.' Should I, or not? Never tried this! Finally, late one night, I rang the number. What would Rita be like? Raunchy or not, she certainly took her time coming to the phone, but – never mind. Perhaps she was finishing off another client before my call. At last, however, the phone was picked up with a click and, to my dismay, an answerphone cut in.

'This,' said an unidentified voice, 'is the debt-collection service for Wigan.'

The second advertisement was more rewarding. 'Four hundred American long-model cornets for sale,' it announced, 'at Gabriel's Horn House, Portsmouth.' Nothing, save Rita, could have speeded my recovery more effectively and a week later I found myself sifting through a gigantic consignment of trumpet-cornets, the rare instrumental hybrid that I've played since 1971. Chris Waters, the proprietor of Gabriel's, had toured America with a wagon and asked every school he passed if they had any old cornets to sell for a few dollars. The practical result was a couple of rooms full of potential cornet-treasures from which I selected a Reynolds Medallist – an American mid-range long-model cornet produced by the firm which also supplied Jack Teagarden with trombones. This instrument helped me through my damaged playing period, standing up to some stiff competition in the process. Only in the year 2000 did it begin to show audible signs of old age. Now I play a Super Olds long-model just as Freddy Randall did all those years ago.

The frustration of not being able to play continued to be simply horrible. For three more years my embouchure was in ruins and even though in 1990 I felt the first beginnings of a return to some form of strength in my lip, it was 1997 before some sort of normality was regained.

During this time, I drank a lot of vodka! But maintaining the appearance of a trumpet-career took sober management and, from time to time, back-to-the-wall tactics. These included issuing records made when I could still play well, with unspecified dates to give the illusion of uninterrupted creativity, avoiding situations that were now impossible (including broadcasting or recording), and regularly using trumpet deputies to get me through testing situations if some unavoidable studio date loomed up.

It seemed that my career might now be over and it was during this time that at least one major reference book – the *Penguin Guide to Jazz on CD* by Richard Cook and Brian Morton – opined that my career had at least 'lost its way'.

Demonstrating the trumpet was impossible for me and this made some areas of teaching difficult too. By this time, as well as working with Stan Barker, I was also hired annually by Dorothy Cooper as trumpet tutor for John Dankworth's eminent Wavendon summer jazz course held at Silsoe College, Bedfordshire. To this course came many of the best young trumpeters in the country in search of improvement – and example! By now I knew my jazz theory to an advanced level, but could very seldom play what I knew, and one day a good young trumpeter put me to the test with a set of written duet studies. After hearing the results, tactfully, without fuss or complaint, he took himself back to evening gigs in London during my week's tenure at Wavendon. All I could offer my students, in truth, was harmonic improvisational opportunities. And, although Dorothy and my fellow tutors were highly forbearing (in fact the problem was never mentioned), it was fortunate that regular broadcasting from 1990 made weeks away from the microphone for teaching purposes impractical for a few years.

One privilege at Wavendon was to get to know George Chisholm a little. By this time, his wife had died and the great trombone master – who could still play with the ease and accuracy of a fine machine – was feeling older and lonely. I had known George for twenty years, ever since I had asked him (tentatively) to come to guest with the Half Dozen at our Southend opening at The Esplanade and had enquired about the charge.

'The fee,' said George, 'will be forty pounds.' This was a lot of money then, and we couldn't afford him but it was plain that this was a fixed tariff and no negotiation was possible.

George was a star – as well as Britain's greatest jazz trombon-ist – and a good businessman.

Later we worked together at the theatre debut of 'Songs for Sandy'. George was still a show stopper but, by now, comedy came slyly through his music rather than via the striped vest and comic routines with which he had starred on the 'Black and White Minstrel Show'. 'If a promoter rings up,' he told me, 'and says, "will you bring the vest and bowler?" I say, "Yes. They'll cost you three hundred extra!"'

This was justified as George had no need to do any more than play trombone for his money. After his master-classes at Wavendon I hardly saw him again and later he was admitted permanently to an old people's home. Tommy McQuater, his colleague in countless projects over decades, was one of his last regular callers. 'I'd ring up,' said Tommy, 'and sing him our old parts from the Ambrose days. I'd sing the trumpet part and George would sing the trombone parts right back.' Life-long friends.

Stan Barker was a rock of support during my period of musi-cal impotence. But by 1987 our time at Southport was over. One of the saddest things about work as a freelance is that it's possible to get used to one place, form memories, plant asso-ciations – and then have them all pulled away again. In Liverpool, our new role in Jazz College was demanding work – music therapy with deeply-handicapped patients – and, to begin with, it was hard to raise any response from our class, many of them confined to wheelchairs, heads lolling. As the weeks went on, however, Stan's bonhomie finally achieved gratifying responses and we had quite a number of our new friends singing, clapping hands, and moving to a simple selec-tion of exercises based on, in one case, 'Organ Grinder's Swing'. To make the tune and the exercises more fun, Stan thought up a Chinese-style introduction.

'Why don't we all pretend to be Chinese?' he suggested, offering a humorous illustration, and was rewarded with a succession of eyes pushed slantwise in spirited impressions of

'Chu Chin Chow'. During the following week several reports reached the Bluecoat Centre of fights in Chinese takeaway restaurants as our students tried their impressions on the street and the next week we were politely asked to leave this exercise out.

For almost a decade Stan and I had been working together. He had endured with fortitude the regular pursuits that took me away from Jazz College. But in 1990, Britain's first jazz radio station, Jazz FM, offered me a weekly show. BBC Radio 2 moved in swiftly thereafter and the direction of my career underwent a change towards London and away from Lancashire. Stan continued working in jazz education, assisted by Rob Buckland, a former pupil at Kent Music School where Jazz College had also operated for several years.

Then, in 1992, I heard that my friend had suffered a stroke. Betty looked after him and Stan worked doggedly to recover his powers of speech and repair his damaged technique. It must have been a long and hellishly lonely battle and, once, he phoned me in tears. But, at long last, he returned to performing and running jazz courses and in 1995 and 1996 we played together again in two happy Christmas concerts just outside Clitheroe. Stan performed magically on these, leading the singing for carols, soloing with the deep feeling that never left his playing and accompanying as only he could. And still he seemed happy to see friends.

Then, on 30th June 1997, I called in to my answerphone to receive some grim, unclear messages and rang back to find out the truth: my old friend had collapsed and, soon after, died. At the funeral, we cast earth on his coffin in a peaceful country corner of the Methodist graveyard near the River Ribble just outside Clitheroe. The memorial service that followed was, strangely, almost merry and Stan would have loved the lusty singing of 'Lord of the Dance' that followed the eulogies and hymns.

I was able to do one last thing for him. Stan had been awarded an honorary degree in music by the Royal Northern College shortly before his death and I knew what this must have meant to this talented – but highly insecure – self-taught musical professional. After he died, a regulation officially prevented the College from awarding the degree posthumously. But, after phone calls and letters, the College authorities graciously agreed to set aside their ruling for an outstanding man. Stan Barker's degree was presented to his wife Betty at an official celebration in 1998 and a great memorial concert was held in his memory at the Royal Northern College of Music. Rob Buckland conducted the College Big Band and students Andy Schofield and Ian Dixon made powerful contributions, as did a galaxy of Barker alumni. It was a lady backstage who gave me my opening line.

'The star of the show couldn't be here tonight,' I said, 'but we hope the deputies will please you.'

8.

radio head blues

Deciding to start broadcasting on a weekly basis for Jazz FM in 1990 (at the invitation of the station's founder Dave Lee) was my most far-reaching career decision since first turning professional in 1977. It seemed like a good idea – a jazz musician with a radio programme should, I reasoned, come to mind more readily than one without, and should therefore perhaps be worth more too.

Not a bad theory, but not necessarily true. Within two years of 1990 – working at one point for Jazz FM, BBC Radio 2 *and* BBC World Service – I found myself with no less than seven regular radio programmes a week. This effectively barred me from almost any other work, kept me away from the cornet (at this point, still a blessing) and drove me into the kind of high-speed production schedule which kept me at home and for much of the time in a harassed frazzle.

My very first moves into jazz broadcasting actually came many years earlier – at the end of the 1970s – with the advent of 'Jazz Score' on Radio 2. I rang the producer Richard Willcox and to my amazement he had heard of me, was immediately friendly, and asked, 'Would you like to come and do a couple of shows?'

At that point, Richard recorded in front of an audience at

the Playhouse, Lower Regent Street, the BBC's legendary home of panel games, variety and 'Jazz Club'. And, while sensible enough to stiffen his panel with experienced broadcasters (Humphrey Lyttelton, Benny Green, Peter Clayton and the invariably hilarious Ronnie Scott and Acker Bilk), he also made it as easy as possible for newcomers to fit in. I, with many fellow panellists, was told the questions (and where necessary the answers!) in advance and even took the precaution of writing my responses down, in the vain hope that our medium-sized audience would somehow fail to see the carefully prepared ad-libs secreted on my lap behind the desk. What I hadn't realised was that knowing the questions in advance was optional. Humphrey Lyttelton to his credit did it the hard way. He also raised havoc,

Peter Clayton

justifiably, before one show by enquiring, at trumpet-volume, 'Right – who's had the questions?' Several fellow contestants, myself included, defensively fiddled with their ties in response. Thereafter – at least for a while – we did it the hard way too, producing unforeseen adjustments in the show's winning form!

'Jazz Score' was no more than an occasional broadcasting treat. My chance to get on the air more regularly had come from another source. One of my initial professional connections in the jazz world, soprano saxophonist Eggy Ley, had stayed in touch after Jazz Legend broke up. He had also continued as fulltime producer for British Forces Broadcasting Service (BFBS) in London and took a chance on me when I asked him about the possibilities of regular broad-casting. My first chance came around 1982 with a six-part series called 'Young Music'.

'You're around the country a lot with Stan Barker doing jazz in education,' Eggy commented. 'You must meet a lot of fine young players. Well, record them and we'll give them a free play on the show.'

This seemed like a good idea but, in practice, recording young players to professional standard in Jazz College's work-shop time was impossible and we ran out of material within a month. 'Young Music' staggered on for its six editions and then foundered. Eggy, despite this failure, was forbearing. 'I'm putting you on a double show with Peter Clayton,' he said. 'It's going to be called 'Having a good time' and all you have to do is play records you like to one another, and say why.'

This ran for more than twenty editions. Peter was literate, funny, had an encyclopaedic knowledge of jazz and popular music, and helped champion my later broadcasting efforts to producer Keith Stewart. With Keith, I depped regularly for Humphrey Lyttelton on his 'Best of Jazz' programme on Radio 2 until 1990 and recorded three series of a BBC World Service show called 'It's Trad'. Eventually this was terminated after the frustrated presenter had stretched the definition of 'trad' further than it could go. 'I'm sorry,' one listener wrote, 'but Bobby Hackett and Jackie Gleason can simply not be classified as 'trad'. Where's the banjo?'

Peter Clayton and I stayed in touch and I got to know him as a friend. If you were introduced to him, he would hold out his hand and say, 'Tall and thin.'

'Yes,' his new acquaintance would say, astonished, 'but how did you know what I was thinking.'

'Because,' said Peter who was short and stocky, 'I've got a tall, thin voice.' My likeable friend was forever hastening from project to project, presenting radio programmes with a grace and skill comparable to that of his hero Alistair Cooke, working on book after book and contributing genuinely witty pieces to everything from national press to in-house jazz magazines at phenomenal speed. According to Keith Stewart, he had once dashed off a weekly column for the *Observer* while on a single visit to the lavatory.

Above all, Peter was preoccupied with the tricks the English language can get up to. It was he who re-invented such new song-titles as 'People Will Say We're In Hove' and 'I've Got You Under My Sink'. It was Peter who dubbed the pioneering jazz DJ, Gilles Peterson (whatever happened to him?), 'Farmer Giles' and who pointed out in the course of one column for *Jazz Express* that 'Eubie Blake shouldn't worry about being 99. If he were in Australia he'd only be 66!' On one occasion I saw his fists tighten because he'd been unable to meet the five-second self-imposed deadline for a *bon mot* on time.

At last, in 1990, came Jazz FM. For several years Dave Lee had been campaigning for a jazz radio station in Britain. Dave had already enjoyed a career as a pianist with John Dankworth's Orchestra and as musical director for Judy Garland and for TV shows including 'That Was The Week That Was'. But during the 1980s he wrote reports, tirelessly haunted government hallways and talked to ministers-in-power, gradually breaking down the layers of natural bias surrounding the issue of a licence for jazz radio alone. 'And,' Dave had promised me, 'as soon as we're up and running, you'll have a show of your own!'

It sounded exciting but I was doubtful until one Saturday night when Dave came to Rayleigh to play a cabaret set between two halves of a jazz concert with my band. Liza Lincoln and I met him in the fish restaurant down the high street and Dave couldn't contain his excitement. 'We've got it!' he told us. 'The franchise! At last! For Jazz FM – our first-ever jazz station. And you'll have that show I promised you, Dig!'

From then on, Jazz FM was big news. Dave invited me to view the station's opulent new premises in a mews close to

Edgware Road: two transmission studios, offices on the first floor and, on the second, a luxurious boardroom and suite, all of which would have looked at home in Buckingham Palace. After my visit, Dave took me for lunch and made the offer. Would I like to present a Sunday lunchtime show each week, with recorded jazz and live interviews?

This sounded great. Live radio, a regular slot and a weekly peak-time weekend show would help what PR people call my 'profile'. And in any case, since my appalling playing problems were far from solved, diversification seemed like a good idea. The only half-realised qualification was that a show such as this was a weekly monkey on the back – interviewees to find, then interviews to plan, themes to conceive, scripts to write and records to select and time out in minutes and seconds. This would take me away from the trumpet but at this point I wasn't sure that was such a bad thing.

Chris Phillips and Jez Nelson (later to present very success-fully for BBC Radio 3) were to handle contemporary jazz and the morning presenter was to be Diana Luke. Helen Mayhew – then a new name, but now one of the station's few founder-presenters still in place – was to bring a new category called 'Dinner Jazz' to the airwaves, Gilles Peterson had 'Acid Jazz' and several other unknown names were inked in on the wallchart. Other expected names, however, were noticeably absent. Where were Peter Clayton, Humphrey Lyttelton, Benny Green and their established peers? Jazz listeners, delighted as they were with the news of their new station, were people with specialist knowledge. Jazz FM's roster of presenters would have to meet this unforgiving firing squad-head-on.

After months of planning, in which everyone who entered the building, it seemed, was given a job and then two secre-taries for luck, Jazz FM was launched in 1990 in a blaze of publicity. Ella Fitzgerald, very old and half-blind, was the honoured guest, and a jam session ensued in which everyone from Steve Williamson to Digby Fairweather had a blow.

Several daytime presenters had simply been asked, 'Do

you like jazz?' at their interviews and naturally answered a fervent, 'Yes!' But right away the mistakes began. One presenter introduced a record, 'by that great clarinettist Bix Beiderbecke'! Another unwittingly announced a record, 'by that great trumpet man Chris Barber.' Ten seconds later, Barber's canny manager Vic Gibbons was on the phone: 'Mr Barber has been playing trombone – for well over forty years!'

'I'm sorry,' said the presenter, 'I'll make a correction tomorrow.' She noted the contents of Chris's musical armoury from *Jazz: the Essential Companion* – trombone, bass trumpet, bass, vocal – and next morning tried to put things right, live on the air: 'I'm so sorry I called Chris a trumpeter yesterday. But of course everyone knows he plays trombone. Oh, and bass trumpet – and bass vocal too!'

'Digby's Sunday Joint', a title that invited raised eyebrows, went out live for the first year of Jazz FM. Live radio was a challenge but my producer was Nick Freeth, a first class professional previously with BBC World Service, and, armed with a script, I got by. Our worst moment was probably just before our very first show. Nick had shown me the ropes in Studio A, pointing out the script rack, how to stack LPs and CDs nearby for his purposes and generally how to set up for a live transmission. Consequently, half an hour before we were due on air, I sauntered into studio A to recreate our rehearsed scenario, arranged my script and records in playing order and, with five minutes to go, went down to say 'hello' to my producer, in Studio B down at the other end of the building.

'It's all set up ready,' I told Nick who was wearing a 'where the hell have you been' look. The look intensified.

'Digby, we're broadcasting from Studio B. That's in *here*!'

Back down the long corridor I sprinted with two minutes to going live-on-air, grabbed CDs and LPs in any old order from studio A and – whoops – there they go, straight on to to the floor. Pick them up, back up the corridor to studio B, hurl the signature tune at Nick, dive into the chair, grab the headphones and in we go. The signature tune went on in the nick of time and, grabbing page one of the script, I spoke my first on-air 'hello' for Jazz FM.

Nick tweaked a studio fader, fell back in his chair and said a very rude word indeed. Then he turned pale, and pushed the fader the other way.

'The whole of London,' he said, 'just heard me say fuck!'

Fortunately his announcement hadn't travelled as far as the airwaves and, after that crisis, the opening edition of 'Sunday Joint' proceeded reasonably smoothly. Nick was an excellent producer, full of enthusiasm for his new project. He also possessed a sly sense of humour. In our early days, I took over live each week from Paul Jones, my long-time pop hero, legendary star of Manfred Mann's group, and by this time a born-again Christian. The change-over involved, literally, slipping into Paul's presenter's chair as he vacated it: a ticklish operation involving speedy movements. To make it easier Nick brought a second chair into the studio. 'Digby,' he instructed, the first time we tried this, 'come and sit on Paul's right hand!'

I would sometimes meet the ever-affable Paul on his way out of Jazz FM, and only once dropped a brick. As his limousine slid to a halt and the window wound down I asked where he was bound. 'Southampton!' said Paul. 'I'm playing there with Keith Smith in two hours!'

'Jesus Christ,' I said inadvertently, the window wound up abruptly and Paul sped away.

Nick Freeth's mishap with his faders on our opening show was only one of many in the history of radio. These self-operated sliding controls, which put broadcasters on and off the air, don't all work in the same direction and consequently have a habit of creating havoc. There's an infamous tale of a BBC newsreader being called at short notice to read the news at Bush House, the headquarters of BBC World Service. Bush House's faders used to move the opposite way to those up the road at Broadcasting House and our luckless friend forgot which building he was in and consequently read the entire news bulletin off-air. The only brief respite came when, having installed a cartridge containing a pre-recorded item, he adjusted his faders the other way to talk to a colleague, inadvertently putting himself on-air for the first time in seven minutes.

'Going out to the chippy John? Get me a large cod and chips, mate. – Thanks!'

There are other famous stories of radio bloopers. The worst and most catastrophic I've heard concerns an announcer who had become a familiar and well-loved voice, latterly on latenight programmes. One night, very late indeed, during a soporific string-laden ballad, he fell momentarily into deep sleep and awoke to find himself running into dead airtime (i.e. silence), the most unforgivable sin in broadcasting.

'Well,' said the unfortunate, snatching himself into semi-wakefulness, 'All you good people out there, I want you to do just what I'm doing. Wake up ... and stop wanking and ...' Unable to locate the seven-second delay button – known universally to broadcasters as the 'fuck' button – the gaff went out over the national airwaves, leaving our discomfited friend short of a gig, as they say in jazz circles.

Interviewing live on air, as I did on the 'Sunday Joint', had its occasional moments too. Many jazz musicians are happier playing than talking about playing. Nick Freeth called this process 'the interview game' and this was something I had to plan for, getting around the problem by painstakingly preparing each conversation, as well as thinking up plenty of reserve conversational gambits long before we went on air. If I failed to do this, anything could happen. One hilarious moment occurred with the delightful (and normally poised) Elaine Delmar who found herself unprepared for a remarkably difficult and silly question. 'Tell me. Who are your favourite songwriters?' There was a short pause while Elaine considered her answer.

'Well, all of them really,' she said. It was my turn for a pause. 'Anybody else?' I ventured. As the perspiration formed on poor Elaine's brow, Nick went to the commercials and we re-grouped accordingly.

Broadcasting bloopers are probably most often committed once the broadcaster is left in midstream without a script. Of course, great performers like Terry Wogan haven't used scripts for years, but lesser mortals including most 'specialist broadcasters', as they're known, usually do. Where possible, to my knowledge, Humphrey Lyttelton has always used scripts written in his elegant calligraphic longhand, and so did Peter Clayton. Looking at what you're going to say normally allows you to catch bloopers before they get past the net. But not always. Just after John Chilton produced his definitive *Who's Who of British Jazz,* I heard myself telling him on the air: 'John, I really enjoyed looking up my own entry!' Ahem!

Jazz FM, starting from big beginnings, quickly ran into the red as well as other troubles. The specialist jazz press made merciless fun of its on-air errors, and the station lost thousands of pounds weekly. Its premises – in a prime London site, littered with attractive secretaries – reportedly required a million pounds a year just to stay open: a dramatic and regrettable contrast to the triumphantly successful Classic FM which, so it was said, had opened in a couple of box-rooms above a disused building in Camden. A few of Jazz FM's less considerate presenters mercilessly used expense accounts and private taxi-hire firms to profligate extent. And, very soon, dismally low listener-figures confirmed the worst. The station, after its opulent beginning, was foundering like the *Titanic* and, one year on (somewhat insensitively) a dis-traught picture of Dave Lee appeared on the cover of *Jazz Express* magazine. But, to generate income, Jazz FM needed major advertisers such as Coca Cola and these employed advertising controllers whose first move would be to check a station's listening figures.

This was the beginning of a terrible time. The luckless Dave Lee and several of the board members left and the fatal words began to be noised abroad: a jazz station cannot work in

Britain. Despite high listener ratings for my show, it was dismissed from the schedules, like several others. Just before we left, the station was taken over by David Maker, late of Birmingham's Buzz FM. Principally with a view to rebuilding the station's tottering finances, he had hired professional staff to produce a 'through the looking glass' version of jazz programming for the station, now to be re-titled JFM.

'Don't the Rolling Stones have a drummer who plays jazz?' was the new angle. 'We can play the Rolling Stones! And didn't Elvis Presley start life as a blues singer? And isn't the blues the same as jazz? OK then...we can play Elvis!'

Such attitudes filled me with steely anger. My principal quarrel was with the Radio Authority – the public body that controls the workings of Independent Radio stations. I contacted the Authority only to be blandly warned that, 'everybody's definition of jazz is different.'

'Possibly so,' I countered, 'but very few people would include Elvis or the Stones.' Our meetings and correspondence continued for some time, and subsequently I wrote an article for the *Independent* that attracted attention. Soon after, a turnaround occurred. My friend, Dennis Matthews, the long-time editor of *Crescendo* magazine rang up. 'Didn't see you at the re-launch of Jazz FM.' said Dennis.

'What re-launch?'

'I have a flyer here,' said Dennis. 'It says that JFM has reverted to a fulltime jazz policy. They've changed the name accordingly – back to Jazz FM. And they're playing jazz too. Here's some names – Zoot Sims, Louis Armstrong, Wynton Marsalis ...'

A perceptive and hard-headed American called Jeannie Bergen had approached the Jazz FM board with a go-ahead proposition. 'Shouldn't we actually play jazz?' suggested Jeannie. 'The music we're supposed to?' The board had stroked its collective chin, decided, 'Yes, perhaps we should!' and Jeannie Bergen had forged ahead. I met her several times and was impressed with her intractable determination, love of jazz and hefty ambitions for the station. She envisaged a

Jazz FM in every region of Britain, paying attention to the local demands of each area and reflecting its jazz scene.

So it was probably not surprising that, soon after, Jeannie Bergen left too and went back to New York for good. Very few jazz musicians – or, indeed, jazz lovers that I know of – even listen to the station any more. But it has created a new audience for 'smooth jazz' and recently a taxi-driver, spotting my trumpet case, asked if I was a musician. 'Jazz musician actually,' I said and my listener's eyes brightened.

'Do you,' he enquired, 'play dinner jazz or smooth jazz?'

My own broadcasting career might have gone on permanent hold. But having scored, to my surprise, a high-ratings success, I was summoned by BBC producer Terry Carter (genially re-christened 'T'Carter and fugue' by Peter Clayton) to substitute for an ailing Peter on Radio 2's 'Jazz Parade'. We had already shared the five-night show for several months when he was unwell and during this more serious relapse I found myself presenting all five nights of 'Jazz Parade', subsequently re-christened 'Jazznotes', for Peter plus his World Service show 'Jazz for the Asking', as well as later editions of my 'Sunday Joint' show, which at the time was still just hanging in there on Jazz FM.

I rapidly found myself racing to meet script and programmatic deadlines. Fortunately Peter was soon back again but progressively he became more ill. During the final months, Terry Carter took a portable recorder to his presenter's home but Peter, supreme professional that he was, struggled back into Portland Place thereafter in a wheelchair until a few days before his death when he was too ill to broadcast at all. It was a dismally undignified end for a broadcaster of supreme skills.

Peter's incomparable talents included a mellifluous voice but my own, by contrast, was going through a far less lovely patch. Some time in the late 1980s, attempts to copy my colleague's conversational inflections had persuaded me to deliver sentences in an unintentionally up-and-down style, bordering on self-parody. I thought it sounded fine and more exciting than my natural delivery, but wiser people thought otherwise and my cultivated style was even described as 'alarming' in the pages of *Crescendo* magazine. The lady in my Westcliff DIY store didn't think much of it either, when I dropped in for a tin of distemper one morning after presenting 'The Best of Jazz' live on air, as deputy for Humphrey Lyttelton. 'Heard you on the radio last night. Doing that jazz programme,' she said. 'You didn't half sound nervous, love!'

If even the DIY lady was spotting a problem, something had to be done and one morning in the studio Terry Carter tackled the challenge, 'We're going to have to get rid of your 'helium factor'. And I'm going to do it. Now let's get started!'

'Hello,' I said, starting somewhere in soprano register, 'and welcome' (now a swoop down two octaves) 'to 'Jazz Parade'.' Terry buzzed his buzzer.

'Do it again!' So I did it again.

'No good! Once more.' And he kept on doing that, until I was so angry I hissed in a malicious monotone, 'Hello again and welcome to 'Jazz Parade'.'

'That's fine,' said my producer, happily. 'Keep it up.'

It was a valuable lesson and gradually I learnt how to modulate and drop my voice for broadcasting purposes. But it took several years before I was happy with the results. Voice production joined the other skills which I gradually learned: how to pace a show, how to take the listener – the one and only listener – into your confidence and how to make your link precisely twenty-one seconds long if that's what's needed.

One of the bonuses of broadcasting was the chance to meet and interview a huge number of major jazz figures, American and British. I came late to this situation and possibly – as friend and colleague Steve Voce once pointed out – had it easier as a result. Twenty years or more beforehand, Steve, Humphrey Lyttelton, Peter Clayton, Alun Morgan and their peers were regularly confronted by the founding fathers of jazz and accepted the gifts or took the flack accordingly. Nevertheless, I found interviewing a demanding responsibility in the early years and tried, wherever possible, to use my own experience as a musician to steer the conversation away from tracks which my guest might find over-familiar.

In 1996, I interviewed Freddie Hubbard. The interview took take place the morning after the last night of his British tour, a night on which Freddie had found himself devoid of lip – and the ability to play the trumpet at all – as the result of a severe infection. Knowing my guest was in the midst of a deeply demoralizing experience (and one that I'd already experienced anyway) I made a suggestion, 'Look! Let's forget about the temporary problems you're having to go through and concentrate on your huge contribution to jazz trumpet history.' Freddie was disarmed and to his great credit talked wonderfully for almost an hour.

This was not, in broadcasting terms, a good thing. Terry Carter rightly complained about being faced with a half-hour of speech that needed compressing into ten minutes. Eventually I learned how to interview by the clock and would make it a matter of pride to stop the conversation gracefully (and, hopefully, without offending the interviewee) on the dot.

Another fascinating visitor to 'Jazznotes' was Artie Shaw. He had come to London to conduct Bob Wilber in South Bank performances of two clarinet concertos – his own, and Mozart's! – and during the course of a short visit garnered almost as much press as he'd done back in the swing-crazy 1930s. Interviewing Artie was indeed, as one perceptive reporter described it at the time, like being a feather in a wind-tunnel. But he talked fascinatingly about everything – from sitting at the feet of Louis Armstrong and his Hot Five when they played at record company conventions back in 1926, right up to the last recordings he himself had made in the early 1950s with a group including pianist Hank Jones. These had just been re-issued and Artie was delighted with them.

Looking back, I wish I'd asked him more about the every-day details of his work. As always, I researched the interview for a week or more but, because Artie is legendarily 'intelligent', decided to ask him questions of the deeper intellectual sort: 'Did being Jewish,' I asked, 'put extra passion in your work?' Plainly Artie had a built-in crap-detector too. 'Bach didn't need it,' he responded. It would have been better to ask this master of the clarinet specifically about his wonderful records with Oran 'Hot Lips' Page or Billy Butterfield, his graceful experiments with strings, or the first hint of rhythm and blues in many Shaw recordings that in some ways made him a rock-and-roll pioneer.

As he left the BBC, a pensioner asked for his autograph and was brushed aside. 'I've never given them!' said the star. 'What use is my name on a piece of paper to you?' Of course that was true. But I was sorry for the elderly man who had asked for such a small favour; he looked heartbroken at the refusal.

We took 'Jazznotes' to New York early in 1996 to do a week of shows from the Apple and on our first night dropped into the Waldorf Astoria where Daryl Sherman, the gifted pianist-singer, entertains night by night. We had met when she came to London a year or two earlier and she had called me up at the suggestion of her old friend and ex-partner, Richard Sudhalter. She and I had done the rounds of the West End record shops and later that night she sat in with my band too, singing quite beautifully. Daryl spotted us as we arrived to hear her at the Waldorf Astoria and broke delightfully into, 'Welcome to New York'. We visited Rutgers University to meet Dan Morgenstern at the Institute of Jazz Studies, where I was able to compare notes about the Institute and our own National Jazz Archive, and blow both Roy Eldridge's trumpet (fitted with a mouthpiece studded with diamonds!) and the silven cornet of Red Nichols.

Best of all, we visited the Louis Armstrong Archive at Queens to view the stock of treasures (including tapes of 800 hours of music that was not available on records) before going on to Louis' house itself. This was for me equivalent to visiting Mecca. In the house – temporarily cleared of Louis' memorabilia – we saw his study with a madonna-like portrait of Lucille, the enormous six-foot bed in which he died, a wonderfully ornate lavatory decorated in silver-lamé, and a downstairs living room where the great man sat and relaxed with family and friends. I shot several rolls of photographs and when finally we left, as the taxi was waiting, took my silver cornet from its case and hit its bell hard against Louis' gatepost – hard enough to produce a visible dent. Terry Carter and his taxi-driver watched uncomprehendingly from the car, but that's one dent I wanted in my cornet, and never intended to lose.

When 'Jazznotes' re-located from London to Birmingham, Terry invited me to make the move too, as 'official presenter'. This was unexpected, even though I took great pride in my radio work. The aim with any show is to make the whole thing sound off the cuff, as well as artistic. But to achieve this result can take days of preparation, thinking up ideas, researching them, finding the right music for illustration, writing and timing links and records and then getting down to the fine points. Will your listener accept two ballads in a row or turn off? Will he or she be disturbed by too violent a stylistic change between tracks? Will the key-change between two segued records sound good, or hurt the ear? And will your listener – please Lord, let it be so! – note the fine conceptual link you've created amidships: such as the musical 'Amen' from Artie Shaw's 'Beyond the Blue Horizon' which echoed a Shavian profundity in our Shaw programme, or some other such.

The answer, in most cases, is probably 'no' – broadcasting is aesthetic fast-food – and many BBC shows are junked after transmission. When Peter Clayton died, the corporation was hard-pressed to find a rep\eat-show to transmit in his memory and the same thing happened after Benny Green's death. A broadcaster's work, however skilled, is seldom viewed as art or even as worthy of preservation. But I pressed on, nevertheless, hoping somehow that a few of the shows on which I had spent time, love and occasionally tears, might find their way into some sort of permanent ether.

On New Year's Eve, 1998, I raced across London to the Bulls Head at Barnes to present 'Jazznotes' live with the band Sax Appeal. The show went well, it seemed, and I took champagne and chocolates into our 'Jazznotes' office in the first week of January. When, jokingly, I asked Terry Carter if he thought I'd be needed after the expiry of my contract in March he looked abashed. 'Well, I didn't want you to know this yet. But there are big changes coming along on Radio 3. The main thing seems to be that they want a woman presenter for the sake of politics. And however good you may be, that's one thing you can't *ever* be!'

True enough. But I couldn't help feeling that, for a specialist show, it was extent of knowledge rather than pitch of voice that should count. The whole situation was a rude reminder of how insecure the life of any media presenter is and, after a temporary reprieve, I was fired, along with several other victims of John Birt's regime, with exactly two weeks to go on my contract. A brief discourteous post-mortem with one of Birt's minions was cut short with my interviewer's well-rehearsed glance at a designer watch. The only comfort was that I was far from alone. Throughout the BBC in 1998, much more established presenters were coming in for similar insensitive treatment and it was a salutary reminder that every freelance should keep his own hands on his steering wheel.

In any case, for some time I had been aware that my career was taking an undesirable, though financially-rewarding sidestep. Now, within two years, as the broadcasting income came to an end, my income would drop by something like ninety per cent! But the endless monkey-on-my-back of four shows a week to research, prepare, script, then record – all of them transmitted at the usual impossibly late hours which the BBC regularly assigns to jazz – was gone. It was time to look back to music, my first love and reason for living, and to look into the future too.

9.

back to the future

During the 1990s, my playing had been slowly recovering some of its old strength. Surgery removed a small benign cyst from my upper lip and gradually, by infinitesimal stages, things began to improve. The process had been slowed by the need to spend days away from the cornet putting BBC programmes together. But, even while the broadcasting was still going strong, I was laying contingency plans.

These still included solo spots wherever possible and regular visits to jazz festivals. These tend to flourish in the most inaccessible venues, a couple of which are in the Welsh mountains: one in Brecon (hugely successful) and another in beautiful Llangollen, the famed home of Wales' national Eisteddfod. I played Llangollen twice, including one riotous session with saxophonist Art Themen and the Pendleburys – Keith (vocals and piano) and Marcia (vocals) – who were joy bringers to any stage, with Marcia's deep-throaty blues knocking out the crowd.

On my first visit to Llangollen I'd packed hastily and forgotten my toothbrush. So, on the first morning, I got up early deciding that if I couldn't brush my teeth at least I could air them with a refreshing walk along the canal that runs above the town. Wandering contentedly along the tranquil waterway, I noticed a figure on the horizon who gradually approached until we were close enough to say hello.

'You're Digby,' said the stranger. 'What are you doing up so early?'

I explained about my toothbrush problem, we laughed, said goodbye and parted. A year later, having been invited back for a second year, I remembered my walk and decided it would be fun to repeat history. So up to the canal I tramped and, as I did so, saw a figure on the horizon, the same person who once again met me at the identical point on the tow-path and this time offered me a small parcel: 'Digby, good to see you again. And, by the way I've bought you a toothbrush.'

Another enjoyable guest-spot at this time was in a Manchester club, Ganders Go South, for trombonist Don Long's band. This spot included a stay at a wonderful hotel which, as one of its principal features, advertised dirty week-ends. The setting was perfect: deep-carpeted halls lined with mahogany manikins, luxurious rooms with jacuzzi, and a bottle of champagne on arrival. But unfortunately I travelled alone.

Sometimes, for a musical breather between broadcasts, I would sit in on Thursday evenings at the Fox and Hounds, a pub in Epping, with a fine team of mainstreamers, amongst them Mike Cotton, trombonist Jackie Free and, on an especially lucky night, Dave Shepherd on clarinet. The two-trumpet format was exhilarating and, one evening, Mike and I casually discussed the idea of a regular group – similar to the World's Greatest Jazz Band of Yank Lawson and Bob Haggart: two trumpets, two trombones and two reeds plus rhythm section. So the idea of an all-star British band – the Great British Jazz Band – playing dixieland and swing was born and I approached my old friend and musical organiser Pete Strange. Pete loved the idea and we assembled a formi-dable team, Mike and I (trumpets), Pete and Roy Williams (trombones), John Barnes and Dave Shepherd (reeds), Brian Lemon (piano), Jim Douglas (guitar), Len Skeat (bass) and Allan Ganley (drums). When I mentioned the idea to old

friend Alan Bates he said, 'Love it! You're signed!' Pete
Strange got to work on the arrangements and the GBJB has
so far made three fine CDs for Alan's Candid label.

Throughout the 1990s, while I was busy broadcasting, I
carried on working in various groups, but most regularly with
the Jazz Superkings. We played every summer for a season of
lunchtime concerts at Broadgate Arena, as well as theatres
and jazz clubs in and out of London after we signed for that
doyen of British agents, Jack Higgins. The Superkings included Dave Shepherd, Al Gay, Roy Williams, Brian Lemon, Jim
Douglas, Len Skeat and, very regularly, Allan Ganley. One of
the many enduring pleasures of working with the Superkings
was to share a stand with Allan – a true friend who knows the
vocabulary of jazz percussion from first to last and has
remained at the peak of his profession since entering it in his
early twenties with Jack Parnell's band.

In common with all my friends in the Superkings, Roy
Williams is a long-term colleague and more like a brother. He
belongs in the international bracket of jazz trombonists and,
like Brian Lemon or fellow trombonist Don Lusher, stead-
fastly refuses to ever say anything bad about any colleague,
under any circumstances. In the small world of British jazz
this is a comparatively rare quality and I once asked in
wonder how he managed it.

'Life's too short!' Roy said with a smile. 'Isn't it?'

In 1998 we embarked together on a jazz cruise for P and O.
The on-board entertainments officer brought his visiting jazz
players together and, after introductions, went through the
routines for shipboard life, emergencies and much else, con-
cluding with the friendly offer, 'so, if there are any problems
amongst you, just let me know.'

'How about the middle eight to 'Have You Met Miss
Jones'?' Roy offered.

Another friend through many years of music making is
bassist Len Skeat. For several years after Velvet we avoided
each other's company. We were two headstrong younger men
then. Later on, when I'd recovered my embouchure and

Roy Williams

confidence in the mid-1980s, I asked Len if we might work together again and when we did we became the very best of friends.

Len is not known as 'The Time Lord' for nothing and, belatedly, he steadily battered into my trumpet playing a sound sense of good time-keeping, an aspect of music often neglected in education but which lies at the very heart of jazz. He also taught me many other valuable lessons. 'If you're faced with something hard to play in a difficult situation, like recording,' he once advised, 'use three words: Stop! Think! Act!'

Len learned his craft in the years of the big bands with their unmercifully high technical standards, strong competitive sense and strict code of professional know-how. His university was the Ted Heath Orchestra where he replaced the eccentric solo virtuoso Johnny Hawksworth. The pressure of working in drilled big bands like Heath's took a vengeful toll on its performers and some, faced with the unremittingly high standards around them, became alcoholics. Len, however, came through triumphant and unscathed. For many years after that, he was amongst the first-call bassists in top-class professional session work, playing for albums, television and film sessions. Such work is similarly unforgiving and Mr Len – as he was once dubbed by a market trader in the Casbah – met its demands with combined musical ability and psychological awareness.

John Barnes is another good friend and I've been lucky enough to work with him for more than thirty years. Back in the late 1960s – when the Alex Welsh band triumphantly visited the Newport Jazz Festival – John was voted new-star baritone in America's *Downbeat* poll. He is a deeply compassionate man as well as an authentic jazz eccentric who loves great comedians and music-hall humour. His monologues (usually taken from the repertoire of Stanley Holloway) are a required conclusion to most of his public appearances, ever since the Alex Welsh days, and on one particularly bizarre New Year's Eve at Ludlow he even decided to alternate between several monologues, stanza by stanza – an exercise in comic surrealism which left his audience a shade mystified.

John loves Laurel and Hardy, and is occasionally filled with the kind of hilarious, short-term fury that assailed Oliver Hardy. Returning from an alcoholic lunch, he decided it was practice time and retired to his upstairs room to play the

John Barnes

baritone saxophone. But the long notes seemed to be sounding ever flatter in pitch, until John, bleary with frustration, raised himself to fury-level. 'There's something wrong with this damn' baritone. I'll fix it.'

And he did, relentlessly sawing half-an-inch off the thin end of the saxophone with a hacksaw. No doubt that would fix the problem! The following morning, he entered his practice room to find the top of his beloved baritone saxophone waving gently in the morning breeze, supported only by insulating tape. 'It's lucky I knew a friendly repairer, Willie Garnett,' I heard him confess later on an edition of 'Jazz Score'. 'Some of the old-school repairers who loved the instrument would probably have thrown me out in the street!'

John's younger namesake and fellow saxophonist, Alan Barnes, lodged with John and his wife for over a year and became something close to a surrogate son to his landlord and landlady. Alan often re-told how, when creeping in late at night past the master bedroom door, he would be greeted with the ritual parental accusation: 'So what kind of time do you call this?'

Such a close relationship certainly didn't harm the one-time rumour that John and Alan were father and son. Humphrey Lyttelton found a neat way to dispel the myth. 'John and Alan are related,' Humph would explain as both men stood alongside him on-stage, 'but not to each other.'

I once asked Alan if he had ever been misbooked in place of John Barnes. He nodded. 'I was down in Wales for a guest-spot,' he said, 'playing with some traditional band or other. And when I opened the door and saw the leader his mouth dropped open! "Oh bloody 'ell, no!"'

Alan knows of other spectacular examples of mistaken identity too and recently told me of a radio station that wanted to book the author Alistair MacLean for an interview. The producer traced him to Canada and received a delighted 'yes' to the proposal. So they booked him and flew him over to record the show. When he arrived, Mr MacLean turned out to be president of a water company.

As early as the start of the 1990s I had become aware of a new malaise. Somewhere behind my activities there seemed to be a need for something new – and for the first time in my playing career, the music that I wanted and needed to play seemed to be changing a little.

A new opportunity opened when I wandered into Dobell's Jazz Record Shop, by then located in Tower Street, to see it in its final hours. What was left in the racks had to be sold that day and, glancing through a handful of videos, I found a set of performances by the Four Freshmen, from bandleader Ray Anthony's television show of the 1950s. I took the video home and my enthusiasm for vocal groups – from the Modernaires via the Freshmen up to Manhattan Transfer – found visual focus. The tape was played and replayed as I recalled the 'Four Freshmen and Five Trombones' album. Wouldn't it be wonderful to have a group that could do that? But I couldn't sing, and none of my present colleagues would probably want to try. For now, it was time just to enjoy the music and dream a little.

Then, in 1992, the Four Freshmen came to Britain to tour with Ray McVay's orchestra. Producer John Langridge was happy for them to appear on 'Jazznotes'. So, one evening, Greg Stegemann and Mike Beissner (two newcomers), veteran Autie Goodman (who had sung for years with the Modernaires) and Bob Flanigan roistered into the foyer of the BBC for an interview. I recognised Bob Flanigan immediately from his appearance on Manhattan Transfer's 'Vocalese' video a few years before. Whereas with the Freshmen in the 1950s he looked like a handsome short-haired college boy, now he sported long curly hair and fashionable glasses. But what hadn't changed was his stature, tall as a baseball forward with the very big feet which back home in America had earned him the affectionate nickname of 'Snowshoe'. Flanigan and all four Freshmen sang like angels at the Queen Elizabeth Hall a day or two later while Liza and I sat spellbound, dead-centre in the front row. This caused mild amusement to my new friends including Mike Beissner. 'Couldn't you get something closer?' Mike queried from the stage.

Once into their act the group ran through many hits including 'Day by Day' with Bob's supercharged trombone solo. Another innovation was their 'Freshhorns' – Autie Goodman, expert on alto saxophone, Bob Flanigan on trombone, Greg Stegemann manning a mellophone and Mike Beissner playing spectacular lead trumpet – all above the excellent Ray McVay band. This was, for me, the opening of another musical door. Musicians who sing are plentiful, but singing in this kind of deeply-ingenious close harmony was something old that was new again. Perhaps one day it might be possible to get together a group that could do something like this. Who knows?

I was becoming pre-occupied with the phrase 'musicians who sing'. I was also thinking that, if the music I loved to play were to stay fresh, I would have to move on and try new things for a while. And, at getting on for fifty, I wanted to work at a project of which I was in full artistic charge. But there were problems, both musical and personal, in trying to enlarge my horizons. A lot of music that I wanted to explore wouldn't interest most of my present colleagues at all. Giants of their craft like Brian Lemon, Al Gay or Dave Shepherd would feel no inclination to turn into barbershop participants at the whim of a junior. But I really wanted to do this! So what was the answer? Perhaps it might be right to go back – at least for some of the time – to my 1970s concept of Dig's Half Dozen, a multi-faceted group that set out to tackle any good music from Dixieland to fusion, except, this time, to make the project bigger and better than first time round.

So, for the first time in twenty-five years, I thought of approaching new players. Trombonist-singer Malcolm Earle Smith, a bright new talent, was one. Next, an old friend, Julian Marc Stringle, who plays saxophones and contemporary music as well as he plays clarinet and dixieland, and who could also sing. I had met Julian in the 1970s when, at the age of twelve, he was leading his own junior jazz band in the Tally

Ho, a well-known jazz venue in Kentish Town. Back then there wasn't yet a trumpet player long enough in the lip to play with the group and I, with some other veterans including Alan Wickham and Alan Elsdon, had helped out.

So who would complete the band? I knew I wanted Bobby Worth, one of the best drummers in the country, who is well-versed in everything from dixieland to jazz-fusion. Finding a bassist was initially more of a problem. After several false starts, in came Len Skeat to set the time, along with guitarist Alwyn Allsop, and we rehearsed a whole variety of new music – even a few revivals from the original Half Dozen's 1971 repertoire!

We played our first dates at the 100 Club, the Pizza Express and one or two arts centres and the band was a revelation. I felt in control, ready to develop my project and happy to make friends with my new colleagues. Malcolm Smith had a serious interest in singing. So did Julian – who similarly sang beautifully – and I was taking vocal tuition. We had already begun singing three part harmony on simple tunes like 'My Monday Date' and had rehearsed a couple of tunes by the Freshmen: 'Day by Day' and 'Time Was'. But, for a while, things began to slow down and I felt temporarily frustrated though determined not to let things slide. Then, one night in 1996, I heard pianist Craig Milverton with Pete Allen's Band and recognised the full scope of his talent as he opened the show with a fully synthesized version of '2001'. Pete was about to reform his band along strict New Orleans lines and so Craig, with his bank of synthesizers, was available to work elsewhere. He could sing too! So Craig joined the band. At this point it leapt forward into top gear and from the first rehearsal it was plain that nothing could stop us. At Clacton Festival in 1996, we rehearsed our four-part vocals on 'Day by Day' and 'Time Was' in the Princes Theatre and afterwards let them loose through a first class PA system at the sun-drenched seafront listeners. At the first note, heads turned and I knew that we were on to something.

Over the next year, fortified by my still generous BBC

wages for 'Jazznotes' (and little knowing that all that was about to end) I carried the band forward, writing new music, investing in a PA system, music stands and much else and assuming benevolent leadership of a project that was all my own. By degrees, for the first time in a musical situation, I found myself observing my colleagues in depth, their ups and downs, their worries and joys. My new band had become a family and in the process I had grown up a little too.

Gradually the Half Dozen developed its set, adding stronger material, honing and pruning, until at last we knew that we had a real show, devoid of standard jazz routines and clichés. It was a fascinating exhibition of musical growth, which carried on as the band moved on and up. Launching any new band has its problems. A few older followers found it difficult to accept the musical diversity of our project but many more loved it. My favourite reaction in the earlier years came when we played the Teignmouth Festival in 1997 and a listener approached me after the concert, 'We came here expecting to hear the same old Digby but this was fantastic! Completely new and wonderful!'

As the song says, everything old was new again.

The band's principal sex symbol was – and is – Julian Marc. Slim and handsome, with hair like Marc Bolan and affable to everyone he meets, Julian is a dish and sports legions of female fans. At one point, early in the band's career, an anonymous well-wisher sent an elegantly-boxed and wrapped red rose to him at every venue we played. I sometimes wondered if some day I might receive a rose too and one evening at the Pizza Express in Maidstone, where I was booked to play solo with pianist Brian Dee's trio, there was an elegant package labelled with my name. Inside it was a rose – and a card.

'Dear Digby, I'm so sorry I won't be there tonight, but do have a good time. And by the way – next time could you bring Julian?'

On Boxing Day 1996, with Beryl Bryden and Nat Gonella, the Half Dozen played a concert for John Woolf's Park Lane

Group to a packed audience in the Purcell Room on the South Bank. We were a successful band and new music was being added to the band's repertoire. I'd even started writing originals which popped into my head and stayed there until they ended up on manuscript paper.

By the 1990s, Nat Gonella had become a good friend and colleague. He had returned to work following the death of his wife in 1994 and in the latter half of the 1990s, heading for his ninetieth birthday, he was still doing the rounds of festivals and concert appearances. At one point he was awarded the Freedom of Gosport and a charming square at the front of the Town Hall was named after him. Later, Nat told Kenny Baker: 'I've had a square named after me in Gosport!'

'That's nothing!' Kenny retorted. 'I've had a street named after me in London!'

Nat had seldom been out of the spotlight after the mid-1980s, when his biography, *Georgia on My Mind*, by Ron and Cyril Brown was published. In a foreword, I praised Nat's originality, star-quality and professional grit amid other admirable qualities. But he never, I think, took himself over seriously. Later I learned that he was just a trumpet player pure and simple, a man who enjoyed life and saw making music as a way to 'pay a few bills' rather than as some high-flown artistic undertaking. Nat tried to explain this to me once. While we were watching the fine trumpeter Cuff Billet playing with his band down on the South Coast, he gave me a nudge: 'Look Digby, that could have been me up there like old Cuff. He's up there with his beer and his fags, having a marvellous time. And that's all I ever wanted to do – see?'

In February 1998 I took part in a new CD to celebrate Nat's ninetieth birthday. It co-featured him with Kenny Baker (a mere 78 years old), Martin Litton, Diz Disley, Teddy Layton and Jack Fallon. And in the same month, my longtime role model joined the Half Dozen for one last week of appearances at London's Pizza on the Park. The club was full of fans and Nat was superb, swinging his effortless vocal way through the set and telling jokes which regularly had both band and audience doubled up with laughter.

One in particular I loved. 'Man walking with his mate along the street and he's got his dog in his arms. All of a sudden the dog goes, "Wuff," and his mate says, "what's the matter?"

"It's alright," says the man, "he just wants to do his business."

So down goes the dog on the pavement and runs over to a wall, puts his front paws up on the wall and does his business, see? Then he runs back to his master who picks him up again.

His mate says, "I've never seen a dog do his business like that before!"

"Oh no, I suppose not," says the man. "But the last time he went, the wall fell on him!"'

I learned a lot from Nat that week: his total relaxation on-stage, his effortless and masterful sense of time and timing as he sang, the microphone held casually at chin-level. Above all, perhaps, I recall his stage deportment: shoulders back and down, stomach discreetly protruding. Ever-aware of the audience, he was master of his stage and it's a vision I shall remember.

For this week, Nat had been billeted out of town in a some-what rudimentary hotel in Hounslow. With his friend and minder John Wortham in attendance to drive and make sure he took his medication, he made the long trip into town each night, even coming down early one day to record a show for 'Jazznotes'. When I queried the long journeys and somewhat primitive hotel arrangements, both John and Nat remained perfect gentlemen, refusing to complain. 'No, mate,' said Nat, 'best not make trouble. It's OK, really.'

On our last night at the club, Nat sang himself to a stand-still and John Wortham and I half-carried him up the steps of the Pizza on the Park to John's small car. As it slowly drove away down Knightsbridge and into Mayfair, I watched the disappearing tail-lights carrying the grand old man back through the high-society streets of his youth. 'Might this,' I wondered, 'be the last time ...'.

I was right. In the summer of 1998 there was bad news. Nat

had broken his elbow and, soon after, he died from a stroke. I was asked to play trumpet and deliver the eulogy for his funeral. This was a test in itself, complicated by the fact that on the way there I found I'd mislaid my mouthpiece and had to use an unfamiliar spare, a risk for any trumpet player. Consequently, I carried into the church, for moral support, a lemonade bottle full of whisky lightly laced with water, and took several deep drafts in the crypt. On one occasion a forbearing vicar passed through and looked the other way.

But then, quite suddenly, I felt a presence. 'Go on, son!' said a voice at my side. 'Go and blow your head off!' Which with Teddy Layton's fine band I did, playing a selection of Gonella standards as the church filled, then 'Georgia on My Mind' as the coffin was carried down the aisle and out to the graveyard.

More than a thousand friends attended the church, including a trumpet-playing contemporary of Nat's – now a Chelsea pensioner – who had been with him at poor-school. Then many of the congregation marched to the graveside where a New Orleans brass band played dirges. Today the grave is marked with a handsome stone with a golden trumpet; all over Gosport there are memorials to Nat Gonella and his updated biography, *The Georgia Boy from London,* is to be published soon by the National Jazz Archive.

In 1995 and 1996, slowly gathering trumpet-strength, I played the Edinburgh Jazz Festival for Mike Hart, partnering American guitarist Marty Grosz in the first year and working the following year for pianist/director Dick Hyman. Dick had been asked to recreate his famous 1974 Louis Armstrong tribute concert at Carnegie Hall for which he transcribed many of Louis' greatest solos for a section of trumpets. At Edinburgh in 1996, two trumpet sections blew at each other across the stage. I had taken the precaution of asking for the music in advance and did some heavy woodshedding, noting with delight that I was playing from the great Pee Wee Erwin's parts, still with their pencilled annotations.

I had met Pee Wee in 1979 at the Capital Jazz Festival at Alexandra Palace, and he had spent far more time than he needed to in making conversation with a star-struck stranger. He had been Warren Vaché's teacher, and his pupil's father, Warren Senior, later helped Pee Wee produce a fascinating autobiography *This Horn for Hire*. I was amazed to find our ten-minute conversation (plus a picture of me) included in the book. That's detail!

In the later 1990s, I played with the legendary Merseysippi Jazz Band, Britain's longest performing revivalist ensemble. Once or twice a year I was invited to travel north to guest with this wonderful Lu Watters-style group and my stopover for these trips was at the home of Merseysippi's cornetist John Lawrence and his wife, Jasmine. To begin with I'd been marginally worried whether I could last the pace, hearing ahead of time about John and Jasmine's celebrated Four O'clock Club, to which you gained membership by staying up drinking whisky until after that hour.

The only time John looked shocked was when – after a late night drink that took us to something after three in the morning – I tentatively enquired if honorary membership of the Four O'clock Club might be a possibility. 'Good Lord, no!' said my friend, as close to outraged as I've seen him; this was an institution of credence and gravity. Clarinettist Dick Charlesworth currently holds the record for the Club, having passed its deadline and drunk on triumphantly to 7.30 before inviting the milkman in for a whisky to start the day!

Another opportunity at this time arose when Chris Walker, who leads a quintet and regularly books me to play, phoned with yet another exciting idea. Would I like to make a cruise on the P and O cruise liner *Oriana* in the equally good company of Kenny Baker leading the Best of British Jazz, trumpeter Bruce Adams' quintet and the superb singer Annie Ross?

I was thrilled at the prospect of meeting Annie again. I'd already interviewed her for 'Jazznotes' and couldn't help remembering a school weekend long ago where I didn't sleep one hour in three nights – all because of hearing Annie's soaring last note at the close of 'Two for the Blues' with Dave Lambert and Jon Hendricks on the classic album 'Sing a Song of Basie'. It was a marvellous bonus to discover that I had a cabin opposite my heroine. But later a cabin-change became necessary, thus saving Annie, without doubt, a good deal of exhausting conversation (ritually known to musicians as 'ear-bending') from her neighbour!

On two occasions on board ship, I chaired jazz discussion groups, one of them consisting only of Annie and myself talking about Charlie Parker before a showing of Clint Eastwood's film 'Bird'. After our onstage chat I sat through two or three minutes of this fanciful movie, then decided to make a discreet early departure and took the ship's lift back to my cabin. One floor down, the lift stopped and in walked Annie Ross – who remembered Bird and Dizzy in person and felt much the same as I did about their portrayal in Eastwood's production.

I did manage to make her laugh once. 'Annie, what do you get if you sing a country song backwards?' She shook her head. 'You get your dog back, your truck back – and your wife back.'

As the century drew to a close, more friends faced the terrifying death sentence that cancer so often turns out to be. Trumpeter Vic Wood, my old friend and inspiration from Southend, collapsed and quickly died. Then in November 1999, coming back from a tour as guest with Carole and Eric Clegg's group Speakeasy, I stopped on Westcliff Station to call agent Jack Higgins from a public phone.

'It's urgent,' said Jack when he answered. 'Kenny Baker is ill. Can you deputise for him with Don Lusher's Best of British Jazz show in Solihull the day after tomorrow?'

I was dismayed to hear about Kenny – Britain's greatest ever trumpeter – and agreed to take the date but then as I walked out of the station I heard scuffling behind me. 'It's you we've

come for, mate,' said a voice and, turning, I saw a flash of silver as a knife slashed my right hand. Two men – one threatening me with his six-inch blade – made off with my luggage
and cornet, while a friendly taxi-driver spotted my plight,
accelerated to pick me up and then gave chase. One hour
later, I was once again on the phone to Jack to explain that
now, minus cornet and en route to hospital, I could no longer
play for Kenny at Solihull.

Four days later my cornet turned up in a second-hand music
shop in Basildon. But, meantime, Kenny was dangerously ill
and had raised himself from a sickbed to play his last engage-
ment of all. His funeral took place at Felpham Church on 22nd
December 1999, a cold, grey and windy day. A New Orleans
parade band led the cortège through mizzling rain, playing
spirituals, and the coffin was carried in through the church's
back door to the muted music of Kenny's band, the Best of
British Jazz. The packed congregation included trumpet stars
ranging from Tommy McQuater to Kenny Ball and Derek
Watkins and there was a moving address from Jack Parnell. 'I
never heard him play a wrong note,' said Jack.

The last years of the century were a sad time in other ways as
Ena was becoming progressively less well. In the mid-1990s
she was finding walking very difficult and came back to live
with me for a while in Westcliff. During this time I continued
playing and writing BBC shows and in September 1998 she
was more or less well enough to move back to Canewdon. But
my mother died in February 1999 and, all in all, the old century ended in tears.

Somehow, amid the sadness, the wonderful things that
could only turn up in the jazz life continued to happen too.
By the end of the 1990s, my playing was back to full strength
after a dozen testing years and my Half Dozen's new album
'Twelve Feet off the Ground' was recorded for Flat Five
Records and received fine reviews. 'There cannot be another
group in the country with this level of versatility,' enthused
the *Observer*.

The Half Dozen celebrated millennium week at Pizza on the Park and suddenly we were twenty-first century jazzmen. Then, in February I was unexpectedly nominated for the freedom of Southend-on-Sea as part of my hometown's 'Millennium Roll of Honour'. To my astonishment, I was granted the award, an honour that remains my proudest achievement of all. Perhaps, I thought, I had done the right thing by going for music as a career all those years ago.

Free at last of the burdens of regular radio and its hazards, I was now a fulltime musician again, in practice and ready to go. Solo work filled my diary, including weeks of guest-spots with Carole and Eric Clegg and Speakeasy. It was fun going back on the road for extended tours of Britain with them.

At the beginning of the twenty-first century, there's still much to be excited about. With my dear friend of thirty years, Pete Strange, I co-lead the Great British Jazz Band: a group of players who are as much musical family as masters of their craft. My own Half Dozen is reaching a performance peak. And, after Kenny Baker's tragic death in 1999, I was honoured to be asked to join the A-team of players – at that time, Don Lusher, Roy Willox, Brian Lemon, Lennie Bush (now replaced by John Rees-Jones) and Ronnie Verrell (now replaced by Pete Cater) – who make up the thirty-year group, the Best of British Jazz. After a lifelong journey it's possible to look around me with satisfaction and anticipation.

Envoi

And that, so far, is the story. I live now in a big detached house in Southend-on-Sea where I can play the trumpet all night. I have loving and understanding friends and life seems to be getting simpler with the way ahead clearer and more creative. But I wonder, does this book, with its light-hearted tales and small tragedies, really reveal what is involved in the life of a fulltime jazz musician? Speeding towards the vocation as a younger man, I felt sure I knew what that was but now, some years older, I am sure of much and of little.

I can't speak for others, but these are some things I've discovered. Playing jazz is tension and release, fear and relief, despair and triumph. It is tenacity, belief and strength. It is being deeply, keenly drunk and bright eyed sober. It is a lifelong passion as consuming as any human love. It can prompt bright elation or irrational highs at one moment, then dark unforgiving vistas of despairing flatlands at the next. Jazz music as a vocation may damage or even brutalize your emotions and responses. Most dangerously, it can remove you from the shores of what people choose to dub reality and can carry you to another dimension from which to view the world at a distance: a world that prompts compliant acceptance or militant irrational rejection as the winds change. Sometimes this Lorelei's only release is the honourable acquittal of a soldier's death.

And jazz – like any popular art – can be a fickle mistress too, casting her onetime loves aside with a fashion-conscious flick of her wrist. Yet somehow the music survives, because – like dance or painting or writing – it offers the eternally seductive gift of self-expression. This is, I think, why jazz musicians carry on. The high euphoria of a fine performance blows away the dawns and days of despair that can follow a bad one more effectively than any fix. And if we forget why we're here, the recorded legacies of our music can relight the candle of creativity that burns inside us all, within a couple of musical measures.

So what can be left behind when all is done? I believe this: that one song, one phrase, one bar, one moment that somewhere causes a heart to move with joy is the only true legacy a jazz musician can leave behind. A brief epitaph for sure but a good one perhaps. And my own ambition? To set free all the music inside me before time is gone. Oh dear Lord, if you will, the time.

Other jazz books from Northway

GOLD DOUBLOONS AND PIECES OF EIGHT
by Harry Gold

The autobiography of saxophonist and band leader Harry Gold – a wonderful memoir of the early years of jazz in Britain

207 pages + 39 photos.

£12.99
ISBN 0-9537040-0-9

BASS LINES: A LIFE IN JAZZ
by Coleridge Goode and Roger Cotterrell

The vivid story of innovative bass player Coleridge Goode who came to Britain from Jamaica in the 1930s and played with Django Reinhardt, Stéphane Grappelli, George Shearing, Joe Harriott, and the Ray Ellington Quartet of Goon Show fame.

£9.99
ISBN 0-9537040-2-5   2002

Northway, 39 Tytherton Road London N19 4PZ. Info@northwaybooks.com